Family Circle

BIG BOOK OF
christmas

GREAT HOLIDAY RECIPES, GIFTS, AND DECORATING IDEAS

A LEISURE ARTS PUBLICATION

Family Circle
BIG BOOK OF
christmas

LEISURE ARTS
Vice President and Editor-in-Chief: Anne Van Wagner Childs
Executive Director: Sandra Graham Case
Design Director: Patricia Wallenfang Sowers
Test Kitchen Director/Foods Editor: Celia Fahr Harkey, R.D.
Editorial Director: Susan Frantz Wiles
Publications Director: Susan White Sullivan
Creative Art Director: Gloria Bearden
Book/Magazine Graphics Art Director: Diane Thomas
Senior Editor: Sherry T. O'Connor

FAMILY CIRCLE
Editor-in-Chief: Susan Kelliher Ungaro
Executive Editor: Barbara Winkler
Food Director: Peggy Katalinich
Home Editor: Lauren Hunter
How-To's Editor: Kathryn Rubinstein

G+J USA PUBLISHING
Books & Licensing Manager: Tammy Palazzo
Books & Licensing Coordinator: Sabeena Lalwani

LEISURE ARTS EDITORIAL STAFF

EDITORIAL
Managing Editor: Linda L. Trimble
Associate Editor: Terri Leming Davidson

TECHNICAL
Managing Editor: Beth M. Knife
Copy Editors: Emily Ford, Karen Jackson,
and Heather J. Doyal

FOODS
Assistant Foods Editor: Jane Kenner Prather
Foods Copy Editor: Judy Millard
Test Kitchen Home Economist: Rose Glass Klein
Test Kitchen Coordinator: Nora Faye Taylor
Test Kitchen Assistants: Brandy Black Alewine
and Donna Huffner Spencer

DESIGN
Designers: Polly Tullis Browning, Diana Sanders Cates,
Cherece Athy Cooper, Cyndi Hansen, Dani Martin,
Sandra Spotts Ritchie, Anne Pulliam Stocks, Billie Steward,
and Linda Diehl Tiano
Executive Assistant: Debra Smith

ART
Graphic Artists: Faith R. Lloyd and Mark R. Potter
Photography Stylists: Beth Carter, Sondra Daniel, Karen Hall,
Aurora Huston, Elizabeth Lackey, and Christina Myers
Publishing Systems Administrator: Cynthia M. Lumpkin
Publishing Systems Assistant: Myra Means

PROMOTIONS
Managing Editor: Alan Caudle
Associate Editor: Steven M. Cooper
Designer: Dale Rowett
Art Director: Linda Lovette Smart

LEISURE ARTS BUSINESS STAFF

Publisher: Rick Barton
Vice President and General Manager: Thomas L. Carlisle
Vice President, Finance: Tom Siebenmorgen
Vice President, Marketing: Bob Humphrey
Vice President, National Accounts: Pam Stebbins

Retail Marketing Director: Margaret Sweetin
General Merchandise Manager: Cathy Laird
Distribution Director: Rob Thieme
Retail Customer Service Manager: Wanda Price
Print Production Manager: Fred F. Pruss

Library of Congress Catalog Number 98-66514
Hardcover ISBN 1-57486-150-6
Softcover ISBN 1-57486-170-0

10 9 8 7 6 5 4 3 2 1

A FEW OF OUR
favorite things

"**M**ade with love" are words that aptly capture the art of crafting holiday keepsakes, and that sentiment is why our *Family Circle Big Book of Christmas* is so special. Whether you are looking for new and creative ways to make stockings or ornaments to decorate your home, or musing about a truly unique item to give as a gift that will last a lifetime, our treasury of crafts will inspire you. In fact, the photo and memory album, at left, embellished with a 1930's family portrait of my mother, her brothers, and sisters, was an especially cherished Christmas present I received last year. I also count as precious many handmade ornaments, wreaths, and painted baskets created by my children, family, and friends. Every year we still adorn the tree with a clay "Rudolph the Red-Nosed Reindeer" my son Ryan made 10 years ago when he was only seven.

Gifts and decorations are only part of the holiday fun. Sitting down and enjoying festive fare, from special dinners and sweet finales to munchies to snack on while trimming the tree, all contribute to the celebratory mood. So we've also included a tasty array of recipes and tablesetting ideas to help your merrymaking along.

We at Family Circle thoroughly enjoyed putting this book together and it is, indeed, "made with love." I sincerely hope our favorite ideas will soon become yours.

Susan Ungaro

Susan Ungaro
Editor-in-Chief, Family Circle

contents

first impressions

GLIMMERING LIGHTS, EVERGREEN BOUGHS, FESTIVE RIBBONS — THESE ARE THE HOLIDAY TOUCHES THAT ADD UP TO A GRAND FIRST IMPRESSION! ACCENT THE LANDSCAPE WITH FRAGRANT NATURALS AND SPRIGHTLY TRIMS AND SET THE SCENE FOR A WONDERLAND OF CHEER.

Nothing captures the holiday spirit like the fresh scent of evergreens. Our delightful candy cane and bell both begin with plastic foam shapes covered with greenery sprigs. Wrap the cane with cheery ribbon, add a clever ornament "clapper" to the bell ... Voilà!

DANDY CANE

You need: 1" thick sheet of 12" x 36" plastic foam; felt marker; serrated knife; fresh evergreens; floral wire; 2 yds of 1 1/2"W red/white checked ribbon; glue gun.

Cutting shape: Use marker to draw a freehand candy cane desired size to fit foam; cut out with knife.

Decorating: Gather small bunches of greens; wrap together with floral wire. Make enough bunches to cover cane. Insert stems of bunches in foam. When cane is covered, wrap with ribbon, tucking in and gluing ends in the back of the cane.

BECKONING BELL

You need: 2" thick sheet of 24" x 36" green plastic foam; felt marker; serrated knife; juniper; white pine; bittersweet; viburnum berries; hypericum berries; green sheet moss; floral U-pins; gold ball ornament; glue gun; 1 yd of 1½"W plaid ribbon; T-pin; picture wire; wreath hanger.

Cutting foam: Enlarge pattern (page 116) to 24"W. Place pattern on foam; trace pattern with marker. Cut out bell shape with knife.

How-To's continued on page 116

For a fragrant cascade (above, left), *twist together a mix of boxwood, pine, and strings of wooden beads. Outline the doorway with evergreens and tie on bright bows (left). The button-eyed gingerbread man is cut from wood, "iced" with paint, and dressed in a ribbon scarf and buttons. An appliquéd banner (above, right) signals for Saint Nick to make a stop.*

Wondering what to do with those old (maybe even chipped) ornaments that you can't bear to part with? Use wire or glue to attach them to a greenery wreath for an "instant" old-fashioned treasure. (Inset) Tiny trims abound with cheer. Fill a little doorknob basket with greenery; finish with a crimson bow.

DRAMATIC DOME

You need: Plastic foam – one 18" dia. ring, one 14" dia. ring, one 12" dia. hollow half ball; glue gun; serrated knife; moss; white pine; boxwood; picture wire; assorted ornaments; floral U-pins; red tassel; 2 yds of 3"W plaid wired ribbon; painter's tape; wreath hanger or nail.

Making half-dome base: Stack and glue plastic foam rings together (small ring centered on top of large ring). Using knife, carve edges so they slant inward (top edges of bottom ring even with bottom edge of top ring). Glue half ball centered on top.

How-To's continued on page 118

To turn your front door into a grand entrance, tie ribbon bows on potted evergreens; hang an exquisite ornamented dome from a length of tartan ribbon.

11

welcome one and all

A FESTIVE FOYER IS A MUST FOR THE SEASON. CHOOSE WREATHS AND OTHER ADORNMENTS IN A STYLE TO SUIT YOUR TASTES, WHETHER YOU PREFER NATURAL ELEGANCE, COUNTRY CHARM, OR GILDED SPLENDOR.

G*ifts from nature — leaves and boughs, fruits and flowers, fresh or dried — lend scent and style to your home. (Opposite) To bring intriguing color and shape to a harvest wreath of fir, pine, and juniper, add pears, tiny artichokes, and baby eggplants. Make a fresh impression with a splendid lime topiary (left). For the banister, simply wire together pine boughs and dot with golden glass balls. Use a metallic marker to write a cheery verse on wire-edge ribbon; stitch the streamer to the edge of a runner, or tie it anywhere you want to send the right message.*

HARVEST WREATH

You need: 16" wire wreath form; spool wire; fresh pine, fir, and juniper branches; wood floral picks; fresh embellishments – artichokes, miniature eggplants, lady apples, Seckel pears; magnolia "skeleton" leaves; dried gypsophilia; 4 yds of 4"W tulle ribbon; 3 yds of 1½"W wired ribbon.

Preparing wreath: Use spool wire to attach pine, fir, and juniper branches to wreath form, overlapping edges to cover wreath completely.

Preparing embellishments: Poke floral pick into base of each vegetable or fruit. Twist wire around leaf clusters and around ends of each pick.

Decorating: Twist each wire around wreath to secure leaves and picks in overlapping rows. Insert gypsophilia into wreath. Tie tulle and wired ribbon in bows. Wire to top of wreath.

How-To's continued on page 120

BERRY BALL

You need: 4" plastic foam ball; 2 yds wide red ribbon; floral U-pins; sheet moss; glue gun; cranberries and other assorted berries; small pinecones; greenery.

Decorating: Fold ribbon in half and knot ribbon together 8" from fold. For hanger, use U-pin and pin knot to top of ball (loop becomes hanger). Wrap ends of ribbon around opposite sides of the ball. Pin ribbon at bottom of ball, leaving ends hanging for streamers; cut fishtail ends. Using U-pins, attach sheet moss to ball. Glue berries to ball. Glue greenery to top and bottom of ball. Glue pinecones to top of ball.

Refresh your stairway (right) by twining evergreen about the handrail, then wiring it in place. Wind with shiny star trim and sheer, shimmering ribbon. Bestow a holiday kiss beneath a berry ball (above), resplendent in emerald moss and ruby fruits.

Celebrate a rich bounty of fruit (left) with a gorgeous circlet of pomegranates, dried lemons and limes, magnolia leaves, and wheat stalks. For packages too pretty to hide under the tree, dress gifts in nature's glory (below): a basket of holly; bouquet of juniper and lavender; cookie cutter overflowing with cranberries; ivy "ribbon"; holly wreath; berry-embellished twig star; ring of pepper-berries; fern frond; rose hip wreath; ivy leaves glued to ribbon; wire basket of lavender and sage.

Fruited Wreath How-To's on page 120

Brilliant berries gleam on an evergreen wreath (right). To make it, tuck sprigs of fir, boxwood, and red berry stems into a twig wreath; finish with a checked ribbon bow. (Opposite) The stunning stained-glass quilt glows as brightly as a church window. Bias-strip "leading" defines traditional motifs on the small quilt. Sew on a rod pocket and hang on the wall, or display on a table.

Stained Glass Quilt How-To's on page 120

The herb-filled sachet (right) features a prized portrait transferred onto muslin. Hang the heart from a doorknob or on the tree — anywhere you want an old-fashioned touch. Punctuate each tip of a pieced star (below) with a button and outline the seams with gold floss.

PORTRAIT HEART SACHET

You need: Photograph; photographic transfer paper; muslin; red velvet; narrow ribbon; fiberfill or dried lavender; greenery sprig.

Transferring photo: Following transfer paper manufacturer's instructions, transfer photo onto muslin. Trim muslin 1/4" past photo edges. Press edges 1/4" to wrong side, clipping if necessary.

Assembling: Use full-size heart pattern (page 122) to cut two hearts from velvet. Center photo on one heart; topstitch in place. With right sides facing and using a 1/4" seam, stitch hearts together, leaving small opening; turn. Stuff with fiberfill or lavender; slipstitch opening closed.

Finishing: Stitch ends of a ribbon length to back of sachet for hanger. Tie ribbon in a bow around greenery; tack to sachet.

How-To's continued on page 122

Take up your needle and thread to create a patchwork wreath your family will cherish forever. For added meaning, choose fabrics and buttons from garments that were once worn by each family member; embroider the names and piece the patches together in crazy-quilt style.

by the chimney

DRESS YOUR
MANTEL FOR THE
MOST ENTRANCING
OF SEASONS. THE
WARMTH OF A
FLICKERING FIRE,
THE SOFT GLOW OF
CANDLES ON THE
MANTELPIECE, THE
STOCKINGS HUNG
WITH CARE — THESE
ARE THE STUFF
CHRISTMAS DREAMS
ARE MADE OF.

Our scalloped stocking (from left) looks sensational in its sprightly scoops. Brimming with gifts, a dish towel stocking evades kitchen duty, and the toile stocking is piped and ruffled in gingham. On a peppermint stocking, red and white disks are button topped and "candily" stitched. Create a wonderfully woolly stocking using sweater remnants.

How-To's on page 123

Celebrate winter's bounty with an abundance of fruit. *For this glowing mantel scene (below), first gather chunky candles in warm hues, circle with ribbon, and arrange with the tallest at the back. Flank with pineapples and fruit-filled gold urns; tuck in pinecones and greens.*

FRUITED GARLAND

You need: Fresh evergreen garland; tinted boxwood; freeze-dried pomegranates, limes, and kumquats; dried orange slices and orange pomanders; dried pepper-berry clusters; clusters of large artificial golden berries; wooden floral picks; 22-gauge floral wire; glue gun; sheer wired ribbon.

How-To's continued on page 124

A swag of greens — ripe with pomegranates, kumquats, and orange slices — can soften a mantel or be draped along a hutch. Wind an airy ribbon through all.

S*tand Father Christmas (above) on your mantel and he'll watch for who's naughty and who's nice. One stocking, finished six ways (right) lets you mix and match styles: Try a cuff with scallops or not, trimmed with rickrack or adorned with holly leaves. As for the pretty pillow, use pinking shears to give it a spirited edge, then stitch on tinkling bells or fluffy pom-poms.*

FATHER CHRISTMAS

You need: Felt – 24" square red, 8" square each white and tan; transfer paper; 5" square cardboard; fiberfill; paintbrushes; acrylic paints – tan, white, black; 3/8 yd of 7/8"W black-and-white gingham taffeta ribbon; 1 yd of 5/8"W black-and-white gingham taffeta ribbon; fabric glue; glue gun; two 3/4" red buttons; cotton swab; cosmetic blush; 3/8 yd of 3/8"W black velvet ribbon; 3/8"W belt buckle; 1/2" white pom-pom; 6" high artificial Christmas tree; 6" of twine.

How-To's continued on page 126

Simple shapes bring cheer to the tree: (Opposite, clockwise from top left) *There's no fancy work needed for a cheery canary; just cut, stitch, and stuff. Fill potpourri hearts with scents of the season. Stitch a crop of everlasting fruit to dangle from the boughs, or whip up personalized envelopes for family members.*

How-To's on page 129

make it merry

A GAILY TRIMMED EVERGREEN MAKES THE
FAMILY ROOM MERRY AND BRIGHT. DRESS THE TREE
IN COLORFUL FELT COOKIE CUTTER SHAPES TO
BRING A SMILE TO EVERYONE WHO ENTERS.

A plain burlap bag becomes a one-of-a-kind gift package for odd-size presents when appliquéd with festive felt firs (right). Complete your tree with a village tree skirt (below). You'll see a Colonial cottage, log house, and steepled church, plus reindeer, red fox, and Scottie pup. (Opposite) This wonderful wall hanging is no-sew! All the felt cutouts are held in place with stick-on adhesive.

SANTA SACK

You need: 22" x 10" piece of burlap; felt scraps – green, dark green, brown, gold; 1 pkg rickrack; fabric glue; buttons; $\frac{1}{2}$ yd of 2"W ribbon.

Assembling: Fold burlap in half, matching short edges (folded edge is bottom); stitch side edges in $\frac{1}{2}$" seam to make sack. Turn under 1" on upper edge; stitch in place to hem. Turn right side out. Cut freehand tree motifs from felt. Glue motifs, rickrack, and buttons to front of sack.

   Finishing: Place gift in sack; tie ribbon in bow around top.

How-To's continued on page 131

glittering gold

FOR A ROOM THAT SHIMMERS AND GLIMMERS,
EMBELLISH THE TREE WITH A GLITTERING GARLAND, THE
TINIEST TWINKLING LIGHTS, AND OTHER RESPLENDENT
ADORNMENTS. IT'S SIMPLE ELEGANCE, WITH A MODERN
TWIST ON TURN-OF-THE-CENTURY STYLE.

Shining pineapples (opposite, left) start as crafts-store wood cutouts, while Victorian balls (opposite, right) are encircled with upholstery trim. Dangling "icicles" are just beads wired together. (This page) Swirl streamers of adding-machine tape covered with Christmas wishes written in gold ink. Swaddle the tree base in a damask skirt.

How-To's on page 134

GLITTERING GOLD

M osaic ornaments catch and reflect every sparkle. Use our easy technique to cut painted illustration board into random pieces; glue the pieces to plastic foam balls, then add deeply tinted "grout" for contrast.

MOSAIC ORNAMENTS

You need (for each ball): 4" plastic foam ball; cold-press illustration board; white gesso; acrylic paints – metallic gold, metallic copper, light red, dark red, light turquoise, turquoise, black; paintbrushes; sponge pieces; faux gold-leaf kit; spackling compound; glossy acrylic spray sealer; craft glue; craft knife.

Preparing ball: Apply several coats of gesso to ball.

Painting: Use craft knife to cut four 6" squares of illustration board. Paint each square as follows: solid dark red sponged with light red and metallic gold, solid

turquoise sponged with light turquoise and metallic gold, solid black sponged with metallic gold, and solid black sponged with metallic copper.

Cutting mosaic pieces: Use craft knife to cut painted illustration board into approx. ⁵/₈"W strips. Cut strips into irregularly shaped triangles and rectangles.

Gluing mosaic pieces: Glue pieces to ball, leaving about ¹/₁₆" between pieces. Let dry overnight.

Applying spackling: Mix black paint with a small amount of spackling until spackling is very dark gray. Use fingers to apply spackling between mosaic pieces. When spaces are filled, use a lightly dampened sponge piece to gently clean spackling residue from mosaic pieces. Allow to dry. Apply additional coats of spackling as needed to build spackling

up to about the same level as mosaic pieces.

Finishing: Follow manufacturer's instructions to apply gold-leaf to some of the gold mosaic pieces. Apply several coats of sealer to balls.

GOLDEN GARLAND

You need: Drill and ¹/₈" drill bit; metal candy molds; gold spray paint; small metal star ornaments; gold spool wire.

Preparing molds: Drill two holes in bottom of each mold, near side edges. Spray-paint molds and stars gold; let dry.

Assembling: To attach each mold and star, thread onto wire. Loop wire through mold holes twice to secure. Twist wire at top of each star to secure. Space molds and stars about 2" apart along length of wire.

*S*pritz candy molds *and tiny stars with gold; link with shining wire for a golden garland (above, left). Glue your treasured buttons of gold and pearl to painted foam balls (above, right) to create more gleaming accents.*

In a flash, you can give inexpensive glass balls and tassels the old razzle-dazzle. (Right) Add instant sparkle with wired-edge ribbon bows and snazzy faux gems. (Far right) Load a glue gun with a glitter stick to add brilliant bands or flashy diamond and star shapes. A glitter pen or iridescent-paint marker will let you draw glistening squiggles or lines here and there. Grab the glue gun again to paste on gemstones or silky braid. For a speckled look, sponge-paint a second glowing color onto gold balls.

nostalgic NOEL

EVOKE MEMORIES
OF A MORE GENTEEL
TIME WITH VINTAGE
PHOTOGRAPHS AND
OLD-FASHIONED
DECORATIONS.
FURBISH THE TREE
WITH CLASSIC
RED TRIMS AND
VICTORIAN-ERA
ENGRAVINGS.
CAPTURE FAMILY
HISTORY WITH TINY
SACHETS, ALBUMS
FOR TREASURED
PHOTOS, OR A
TARTAN-RUFFLED
CUSHION.

"ENGRAVED" PLAQUES

You need (for each plaque): Drill and 1/8" drill bit; small wood plaque; paintbrush; acrylic paints – red, sienna, umber; gold-leaf paint; black-and-white photocopy of simple drawing; matte acrylic sealer; 1/2 yd of 1/8"W ribbon; wire ornament hanger.

Preparing ornament: Drill hole near top of plaque. Paint red; let dry. Apply gold leaf to edges.

Decoupaging: Cut motif from photocopy. Coat back of motif with sealer; press into position on ornament.

Finishing: Coat ornament with sealer; let dry. Tint small amount of sealer with sienna and umber paints for aged look; coat with tinted sealer. Thread ribbon through hole in ornament and tie bow. Slip hanger through back of bow.

PORTRAIT SACHETS

You need (for each sachet): Photograph; iron-on photo transfer paper; iron; three 8" squares of muslin; fiberfill or dried lavender; and optional solid color fabric scrap or purchased welting.

Transferring photo: Following transfer-paper manufacturer's instructions, transfer photo onto one muslin square. Trim muslin 1/4" past photo edges. Turn under 1/4" on edges, clipping if necessary, and press.

Making pillow front: If desired, cut a shape from fabric scrap 1/2" larger than photo. Turn under 1/4" on edges, clipping if necessary, and press. Pin photo (and optional fabric shape) to another muslin square, right sides up. Topstitch photo edges to make pillow front.

Assembling: If desired, match edges and baste welting to right side of pillow front. Pin remaining muslin square to pillow front, right sides facing. Stitch edges in 1/4" seams, leaving opening along one side. Turn right side out; stuff. Slipstitch opening closed.

MEMORY ALBUMS

You need: Photo album with window opening on front cover; 1 1/2 yds of 1/2"W ribbon; fabric glue.

Assembling: Glue ribbon to edges of window opening, turning end under at first corner and forming miters at each corner. Remove existing ribbon ties from album. Cut two 12" pieces of ribbon. Glue each ribbon at old tie position.

TARTAN-RUFFLED CUSHION

You need: Photograph; iron-on photo transfer paper; iron; 16" square of muslin; air-soluble fabric marker; three 16" squares of linen; 5 yds of 3 1/2"W ribbon; fiberfill.

Transferring photo: Following transfer-paper manufacturer's directions, transfer photo onto center of muslin square.

How-To's continued on page 134

presents with presence

THERE'S ALWAYS A LITTLE EXTRA LOVE INSIDE THE
PACKAGE WHEN YOU'VE MADE THE PRESENT YOURSELF.
UNIQUE TOYS, FESTIVE SWEATERS, JOLLY HOME
ACCESSORIES, AND CRAFTY WRAPPINGS ARE SURE TO BE
CHERISHED WHEN THEY'RE FROM HEART AND HAND.

Create a cuddly bear pair in plush felt: Adorable!
(Opposite, from left) Put a real sled to indoor use
as a shelf for stowing packages near the tree.
Embellish plain brown paper with pinecone
stamps, sprigs of evergreen, or other
wintry images.

How-To's on page 135

PRESENTS WITH PRESENCE

There's something perfect for everyone on your list: Kraft paper boxes stack up to create these engaging personalities (below). For Christmas-cottage bags to hold goodies (opposite, top), roof lunch bags with folded paper. (Opposite, bottom) Special surprises for loved ones will look festive in felt bags tied with reindeer and Santa ornaments.

TARTAN ELF

You need: Set of 3 graduated-size oval Kraft paper boxes; two 1$\frac{1}{2}$" wood circles; 1" wood knob; paintbrushes; primer; sandpaper; acrylic paints – red, blush, black, white; glue gun; 1 yd tartan flannel; red thread; tissue paper; 19 jingle bells; 24" of red prairie-point trim; two $\frac{5}{8}$" wood buttons.

Preparing pieces: Prime small and medium boxes, lid from medium box, wood circles, and knob. Sand wood pieces.

Making head: Paint half (back) of small box black. Paint front of box and wood circles (cheeks) blush. Shade outer edges of cheeks with red. When dry, paint red spirals on cheeks. Blend blush and red;

paint knob (nose). Mark cheek and nose placement on face. Paint eyes black and mouth red. Highlight eyes, cheeks, and nose with white. Dry-brush black hair around face. Glue on cheeks and nose.

Making hat: Cut tartan rectangle 18$\frac{1}{2}$" x 25". Glue short edges together to form a tube. Cut 2" fringe at one edge. Slip unfringed edge of tube over small lid lip, folding edge $\frac{1}{4}$" inside; glue. Stuff tube lightly with tissue paper; gather fringe; wrap with thread, just under fringe. Sew two bells at fringed end. Glue hat on head.

Making body: Paint medium box and lid red. Glue lid on box. Mark two 1$\frac{1}{4}$"W suspenders (2$\frac{3}{4}$" apart); paint black. Sew bells to prairie points.

How-To's continued on page 136

These frosty-looking gifts radiate holiday warmth: The painted glass "snowball" (right) is a terrific way to show your love. The cozy crocheted afghan (below) makes a great winter wrap. (Opposite) A plumply stuffed snowman sews up in a snap from soft polar fleece. What an irresistible keepsake!

HEARTWARMING "SNOWBALL" ORNAMENT

You need: iridescent white glass ornament; paint pens – red, green, black.
To do: Use green paint pen to write "You melt my" on ornament. Use black paint pen to draw a heart, heart rays, and snowflakes. Fill in heart using red paint pen.

How-To's continued on page 138

CROSS-STITCHED ORNAMENTS

You need (for each): 8" square of 14-count white perforated plastic; DMC embroidery floss (see key, page 140); 8" of ¹/₈"W ribbon; white paper; craft glue.

Stitching: *Use 3 strands of cotton floss and 2 strands of metallic floss for cross stitches. Use 2 strands of floss for backstitches. Work quarter stitches using full cross stitches of your color choice.* Stitch desired ornament design on plastic, following chart (page 140). Work long stitches within points of star ornament or Algerian eye stitches within other ornaments using 2 strands of floss.

Finishing: Cut out ornament one thread away from edges of design. Glue ends of ribbon to back of ornament for hanger. Glue ornament to paper. Trim paper even with ornament edges.

ORNAMENTS CUSHION

Size: 16" x 16"

You need: 18" square of 18-count white cross-stitch fabric; DMC embroidery floss (see key, page 140); embroidery hoop; ¹/₂ yd fusible fleece; 2 yds decorative cord (with attached fabric lip); 18" square of fabric (backing); fiberfill.

Stitching: *Use 4 strands of cotton or metallic floss for cross stitches and 2 strands of floss for backstitches.* Stitch design over two fabric threads, following chart (page 140). Work long stitches within points of star ornament and Algerian eye stitches within other ornaments, using two strands black floss.

Finishing fabric: Cut two 18" squares of fleece. Fuse fleece to wrong side of pillow top and fabric backing. Trim pieces to 17" x 17".

Making pillow: Pin cord around right side of top, raw edges even; stitch. Pin backing to top, right sides facing, cord inside "sandwich." Stitch; leave opening. Turn; stuff; stitch closed.

PRESENTS WITH PRESENCE

Candles studded with gold will give off twice the glow (opposite, bottom). *Just glue tiny golden half-beads onto fragrant pillars in assorted rich colors and arrange them on a festive tray. Captured in cross stitch (below and opposite), the motifs on these opulent ornaments and cushion glimmer with bright metallic threads.*

Change plain store-bought sweaters into charming gifts with quickie add-ons! Seems incredible, but all you do to create these kicky knits is glue trims this way and that on plain, inexpensive pullovers and cardigans.

How-To's on page 142

SOCK REINDEER

You need: Infant's or toddler's sock, size 4/5 or smaller; fiberfill; 12" of ¼" dia. dowel; fabric glue; 2 twigs; 2 black beads; two ¼" wood buttons; leather remnant; small amount of Spanish moss; ¾ yd leather lacing.

Note: Reindeer toy is not intended for children 3 years and under.

Assembling: Sew running stitches 1" from open end of sock. Stuff sock with fiberfill. Fold dart in each side of sock to shape neck; stitch dart. Place sock on dowel. Pull up threads to secure sock to dowel. Apply glue under gathered area to secure sock to dowel, forming toy.

Finishing: Cut two small slits in top of head. Dip end of each twig in glue;

insert into holes, forming antlers. Sew on button and beads for eyes. Cut two small triangles from leather; fold and glue at base to form ears. Glue ears to head. Glue moss to top of head between ears. Glue lacing around mouth and head for bridle. Glue ends of remaining lacing to sides of bridle for reins.

BABY'S FIRST CHRISTMAS FRAME

You need: 5" x 6" wooden craft frame with 2" x 3" opening; crafting foam – red, brown, white, green, yellow, blue; acrylic paints – beige, yellow; paintbrushes; hole punch; glue gun; fine-point black permanent marker.

Cutting: Use full-size patterns (page 143) to cut out following crafting foam pieces: green tree pieces, yellow star, red dress, white body, brown hair. Use hole punch to cut out following crafting foam circles: three white, four green, three yellow, four red, three blue.

Painting: Paint frame yellow. Paint face, hands, and feet on body beige following pattern.

Finishing: Glue star to red crafting foam. Cut out foam slightly larger than star. Glue foam pieces to frame. Use marker to write "Baby's 1st Christmas" on frame and draw eye on angel.

ELF PUPPETS

You need (for both): Felt – three 9" x 12" pieces red, two 9" x 12" pieces each green and yellow, one 9" x 12" piece each cream and light tan, one 4" square pink; craft glue; yarn – brown,

How-To's continued on page 144

It's child's play to make reindeer magnets by gluing chenille stems, pom-poms, and wiggle eyes to walnut shells (above, from top left). For baby's frame, glue on Christmas cutouts of colorful craft foam. Youngsters can put on their own holiday show with a set of Santa's helpers in "hand-y" shapes. (Opposite) Turn a toddler's footgear into twig-antlered stick "ponies" for plant pokes or party favors.

Deliver sweet wishes with a basket of gingerbread people and a cross-stitched message. (Opposite) These jaunty gents will enchant anyone: Knit the ginger doll (top right) in his holiday best. Stitch his stuffed pal from wool suiting, and bundle him in a ski hat and scarf. Give each ginger kid a dapper vest.

SWEET NOEL BASKET

You need: 1 recipe of Gingerbread Cookie Mitts Dough (page 94); ³/₄"W heart cookie cutter; drinking straw; fork; acrylic paints – red, black; paintbrush; 10" x 12" wall basket; two 7" x 10" pieces of 14-count cross stitch fabric; DMC embroidery floss (see key, page 145); fiberfill; 10" of ³/₈"W red grosgrain ribbon; artificial greenery; raffia; glue gun.

Note: This is a decorative project and should not be eaten.

Making gingerbread people: Heat oven to 325°. On a lightly floured surface, roll out one-half of chilled dough to ³/₈" thick. Use full-size pattern (page 145) to cut out two ginger boys. Cut out remainder of dough as desired. Spray cookie sheet with non-stick vegetable-oil cooking spray. Transfer ginger boys to cookie sheet. Use fork, cookie cutter, and straw to lightly imprint dough as desired. Bake 30 to 35 minutes or until lightly browned.

How-To's continued on page 145

terrific tables

SERVE UP YULETIDE SPIRIT IN THE DINING ROOM
WITH EDIBLE DECORATIONS AND FESTIVE PLACE
SETTINGS. DON'T FORGET TO ADD HOLIDAY
TOUCHES TO HUTCHES AND WALLS, TOO!

Start the celebration by setting the table with holiday mugs and ruby and emerald goblets (opposite). Finish the scene by dressing up chairs with folksy gingham pads. For a centerpiece treat, spruce up a wooden tree with tiny cookies and the cutters, too! (Below) The gingerbread cottage, paved with peppermints, looks good enough to eat.

How-To's on page 150

NO-SEW ADVENT BANNER

You need: 17" x 29^1/$_2$" piece of white canvas; 1"W fusible web tape; 3^1/$_4$ yds of 1"W green grosgrain ribbon; 2 yds of 1^1/$_2$"W red satin ribbon; tracing paper; transfer paper; red plaid fabric; paper-backed fusible web; red fabric marker; black permanent medium-point marker; 7 yds of ^{1}/$_8$"W red satin ribbon; large embroidery needle; 24 wrapped disk candies; 2" dia. jingle bell; glue gun; assorted buttons.

Making banner: Mark center of one short edge (bottom) of canvas. Make a mark on each side edge 21" from top. Draw lines, connecting marks, to form a point. Cut along drawn lines. Use web tape to make 1"W hems on each edge of banner, trimming at points and corners as needed.

Adding ribbon borders: Fuse web tape to one side of 1"W ribbon. Fuse a 14" ribbon length across banner 9^1/$_4$" from top edge. Overlapping and trimming ends to fit, fuse ribbon ^{1}/$_4$" from edges of banner.

Decorating banner: Trace full-size "Hurry Santa!" pattern (page 152) onto tracing paper. Use transfer paper to transfer design onto banner. Trace full-size heart patterns (one large and two small) (page 152) onto paper side of web. Fuse web to wrong side of plaid fabric. Cut out hearts. Fuse hearts to banner. Use red fabric marker to fill in letters. Use black marker to outline letters, draw "stitches" along inside edges of each banner section, and draw "stitches" on hearts. Glue buttons to banner.

Adding candy: To mark positions for candy placement, begin 1^1/$_4$" from side ribbon and 1" below center ribbon. Mark six points 2" apart. Working 2" below previous marks, repeat for three more rows. Use needle to thread a 10" length of ^{1}/$_8$"W ribbon through banner at each mark. Tie candy to each ribbon length.

How-To's continued on page 152

The message on this no-sew countdown calendar (opposite) needs no explanation! Kids will enjoy marking off each day until Christmas with a tasty treat. Candies make a colorful kissing ball (left). Glue peppermints to a foam ball, then add red and green candies on top. Here's a sweet and simple way to store holiday goodies (below): Dress up clear jars with bits of ribbon and pictures cut from greeting cards.

Kissing Ball How-To's on page 153

Spread cheer with trims and treats in candy-cane colors. A redwork ornament (above) can hang anywhere — in a window, on a knob, on a chair. Add stripes to flowerpots and polka-dots to a teapot (right); display on shelves lined with a punched-paper border. (Opposite) Dress the table with a scalloped runner. Stacked cake stands and glasses make a perfect display (secure glassware with bits of floral clay.) Include frosted glass votives, tissue paper crackers, and all your favorite red and white treats. Round out the decor with goody globes (for display, not eating!). Just glue tissue paper, then candies over foam balls.

How-To's on page 153

TERRIFIC TABLES

If Santa's coming to supper, what better centerpiece (opposite) *than a hand-painted sleigh overflowing with gifts! Wooden star-shaped candle holders are gussied up with fabric and paint. Wintry pinecones decorate the chairs. (Below) Napkin rings made of real birch bark double as place cards when names are added using a woodburning tool.*

How-To's on page 155

TERRIFIC TABLES

PLACE-CARD HOLDER

You need: Newspaper; small (soup) can; gold spray paint; silk leaves; glue gun; 28" of 1½"W gold ribbon; roses; pinking shears; paper.

To do: Protect work area with newspaper. Spray-paint can. Spray-paint both sides of leaves, cutting stems off if necessary. When dry, glue leaves around can. Wrap with ribbon; tie bow. Fill with roses. For place card, pink edges of 2" x 3" piece of paper; write name. Tuck card between roses.

GALA GOBLETS

You need: Glass goblets; paintbrushes – ¾" flat, small liner; surface conditioner for permanent craft enamel paints; ¾"W

masking tape; permanent black marker (fine point); permanent enamel craft paint – red, green, metallic gold; gloss glaze for permanent enamel craft paints.

Preparing: Wash/dry goblets. Brush outside with surface conditioner.

Painting: *Stripes* – Adhere tape around goblet, about midway up bowl. With marker, dot guide marks on bowl along both edges of tape. Remove tape. Paint a gold stripe between marks, and a ¾"W gold stripe around edge of base. **Holly** – Paint freehand leaves along stripes. Dot on berries.

Finishing: When dry, apply gloss glaze on painted areas only.

The prettiest place setting (opposite) includes a place-card holder filled with fragrant roses. Tie strands of golden beads and a shimmering ribbon around each napkin. Yuletide toasts will be even more memorable with gala goblets (below, left) — glass stemware painted freehand. A baubled bell jar sparkles on the sideboard. Simply hold a jar (or a cake cover) upside down and have a helper fill it with colorful balls. Next, place a plate over the opening and turn jar right side up.

61

festive feasts

WITH FIXINGS
BOTH SAVORY AND
SWEET, THESE TWO
TEMPTING DINNERS
ARE SURE TO PLEASE
GUESTS. AND SINCE
SOME DISHES ARE
MAKE-AHEAD,
YOU'LL HAVE MORE
TIME TO ENJOY
YOURSELF.

MENU I

SMOKED TROUT CANAPÉS

SALMON CANAPÉS

WINTER BISQUE
WITH CHIVE-CREAM SWIRL

CITRUS GAME HENS
WITH ROASTED POTATOES

MIXED MARINATED
VEGETABLES

MULTIGRAIN
BUTTERMILK ROLLS

HOLIDAY UPSIDE-DOWN CAKE

CAPPUCCINO MOUSSE PIE

MENU II

PESTO-RED PEPPER
CREAM SPREAD

CHICORY SALAD

CASSIS-GLAZED BAKED HAM

ROASTED POTATOES WITH
GARLIC AND ROSEMARY

VEGETABLE TIAN

CAULIFLOWER GRATIN

STRING BEANS PROVENÇAL

HOLIDAY VENETIANS

WINTER BISQUE WITH CHIVE-CREAM SWIRL

Bisque:

 2 butternut squash (3 pounds)
 1 large sweet potato, unpeeled, quartered lengthwise
 1 red onion, unpeeled, ends trimmed and quartered
 4 cloves garlic, unpeeled
 2 cans (13¾ ounces each) reduced-sodium chicken broth
 2 tablespoons chopped fresh sage OR ½ teaspoon dried leaf sage, crumbled
 1½ teaspoons salt
 ½ teaspoon hot-pepper sauce

Chive Cream:

 1 small bunch chives, cut into 2-inch lengths (⅓ cup)
 ½ cup sour cream
 ½ cup half-and-half
 Chives, for garnish (optional)

1. Prepare Bisque: Heat oven to 450°. Coat roasting pan with nonstick vegetable-oil cooking spray.
2. Halve squash lengthwise; remove seeds. Cut halves in half crosswise. Place squash, potato, onion, and garlic in pan. Cover tightly with foil.
3. Bake in 450° oven 55 to 60 minutes or until tender. (To microwave, place vegetables in microwave-safe 13 x 9 x 2-inch baking dish. Cover tightly with plastic wrap. Microwave at 100% for 20 minutes. Carefully uncover.) When cool enough to handle, scoop flesh from squash and potato; remove skins from onion and garlic. Place cooked vegetables in food processor. Whirl until smooth.
4. Combine purée, broth, sage, salt, and pepper sauce in saucepan. Simmer 5 minutes. (Can be made up to this point a day ahead; refrigerate.)
5. Prepare Chive Cream: Chop chives in food processor. Add sour cream. Whirl until blended. (Can be made 3 hours ahead; refrigerate.)
6. To serve, heat soup. Stir in half-and-half; gently heat through. Spoon into bowls. Drizzle Chive Cream over top. Garnish with chives, if desired.
Yield: Makes 8 servings.

SMOKED TROUT CANAPÉS

 1 loaf Italian bread (18 inches), cut into about thirty-two ½-inch-thick slices
 2 tablespoons butter, melted
 3 tablespoons sour cream
 1 teaspoon prepared horseradish
 ⅛ teaspoon salt
 2 heads Bibb lettuce
 6 to 8 ounces smoked trout fillet, skinned, bones removed, and cut into 1-inch pieces
 ¼ sweet red pepper, cored, seeded, and cut into ½-inch diamonds, for garnish

1. Heat oven to 400°.
2. Lightly brush both sides of bread slices with melted butter. Place in single layer on baking sheet.
3. Bake in 400° oven for 8 minutes or until the bread slices turn golden brown, turning each slice over after the first 4 minutes.

*C*ornish hens (opposite), *glazed with citrus sauce and served with crispy roasted potatoes, make an enticing entrée. Oven-warm rolls are flecked with oats. Bake them the day before and reheat. (Above)* Sage and a hint of hot-pepper sauce round out the flavor of a creamy winter squash bisque.

3. Bake in 400° oven for 8 minutes or until the bread slices turn golden brown, turning each slice over after the first 4 minutes.

4. Stir together the sour cream and honey mustard in a small bowl until well blended. Brush one side of each piece of toast with honey-mustard mixture. Arrange toast pieces, mustard side up, on serving platter.

5. Carefully select blemish-free inner leaves from the heads of the Bibb lettuce. (Reserve remainder of heads for salad.) Trim leaves so they fit neatly on top of bread slices. Place 1 leaf on each bread slice.

6. Cut salmon into 2½ x 1-inch strips. Roll up each strip loosely and shape to form rose. Place 1 rose on each lettuce leaf. Garnish with dill.

Yield: Makes 32 canapés.

*F*inger foods are perfect for an informal party. Guests will help themselves to savory smoked trout or salmon canapés. (Opposite) Oil-cured olives dot a medley of tangy marinated vegetables. Prepare the salad a day ahead and bring to room temperature to serve.

4. Stir together the sour cream, horseradish, and salt in a small bowl until well blended.

5. Carefully select blemish-free inner leaves from the heads of the Bibb lettuce. (Reserve remainder of heads for salad.) Trim leaves so they fit neatly on top of bread slices. Place 1 leaf on each bread slice. Top each with a piece of trout and a dollop of the horseradish mixture. Garnish each canapé with a sweet red pepper diamond.

Yield: Makes 32 canapés.

SALMON CANAPÉS

1 loaf Italian bread (18 inches), cut into about thirty-two ½-inch-thick slices
2 tablespoons butter, melted
2 tablespoons sour cream
1 tablespoon honey mustard
2 heads Bibb lettuce
8 ounces smoked salmon, sliced
1 bunch fresh dill, for garnish

1. Heat oven to 400°.
2. Lightly brush both sides of bread slices with melted butter. Place in single layer on baking sheet.

CITRUS GAME HENS WITH ROASTED POTATOES

Cornish Hens:

4 Cornish hens (about 1¼ pounds each)
¼ cup orange juice concentrate
¼ cup fresh lemon juice
3 tablespoons chili sauce
2 tablespoons Worcestershire sauce
2 tablespoons honey OR sugar
2 tablespoons fresh thyme OR 1½ teaspoons dried leaf thyme, crumbled

Potatoes:

1 pound red potatoes, unpeeled, cut into large cubes
1¼ pounds sweet potatoes, unpeeled, cut into large cubes
¾ pound shallots, peeled
3 tablespoons olive oil
¼ cup fresh thyme OR 1 tablespoon dried leaf thyme, crumbled
1¼ teaspoons kosher (coarse) salt OR regular salt
1¼ teaspoons ground black pepper
2 tablespoons cornstarch, dissolved in 2 tablespoons cold water
Fresh thyme sprigs and lemon and orange slices, for garnish

1. Prepare Cornish Hens: Split hens down center. Place hens, skin side down, in two 13 x 9 x 2-inch baking dishes.

2. To make marinade, combine juice concentrate, lemon juice, chili sauce, Worcestershire, and honey in bowl. Pour evenly over hens in baking dishes. Cover hens and refrigerate for up to 1 day, turning occasionally. (Can be frozen for up to 1 month; thaw in refrigerator before using.)

3. Remove hens from refrigerator 1 hour before cooking. Turn hens, skin side up, in dishes; brush with marinade in dishes. Sprinkle on thyme.

4. Prepare Potatoes: Toss red and sweet potatoes, shallots, oil, thyme, 1 teaspoon coarse salt, and pepper in bowl. Place in foil-lined roasting pan.

5. Heat oven to 400°. Place potatoes on upper rack and hens on middle rack in oven. Bake for 40 minutes or until vegetables are fork-tender and meat is no longer pink near bone (185° on instant-read meat thermometer). Stir potatoes and baste hens with marinade halfway through cooking. Transfer hens and potato mixture to platter; cover and keep warm.

6. Prepare sauce: Strain cooking juices from hens into 4-cup glass measure; defat (you should have 1 cup juices; add water or chicken broth to equal 2 cups). Place in saucepan with remaining ¹/₄ teaspoon salt. Bring to boiling. Stir in dissolved cornstarch mixture. Boil, stirring, until thickened, about 1 minute.

7. Garnish hens with thyme, lemon, and orange. Serve with sauce.

Yield: Makes 8 servings.

MIXED MARINATED VEGETABLES

Salad:

- 1 small head cauliflower, cut into small flowerets (5 cups)
- 2 stalks broccoli, cut into small flowerets (4 cups)
- 4 thin carrots, sliced diagonally
- 1 sweet yellow pepper, cut into 2 x ¹/₂-inch strips
- ¹/₂ cup pitted oil-cured black olives

Dressing:

- ¹/₂ cup olive oil
- 3 tablespoons fresh lemon juice
- 2 tablespoons balsamic vinegar
- 2 teaspoons Dijon-style mustard
- 1¹/₂ teaspoons salt
- ¹/₄ teaspoon ground black pepper
- ¹/₄ cup finely chopped parsley
- 3 green onions, finely chopped

1. Prepare Salad: Cook cauliflower in boiling water 2 minutes. Add broccoli and carrot; cook 3 minutes. Add yellow pepper; cook 3 to 4 minutes or until vegetables are tender-crisp. Drain; rinse under cold running water. Place in serving bowl with olives.

2. Prepare Dressing: Whisk oil, lemon juice, vinegar, mustard, salt, and pepper in bowl. (Can be made 8 hours ahead; cover and refrigerate.)

3. To serve, toss vegetables, dressing, parsley, and green onion. Serve at room temperature or chilled.

Yield: Makes 8 servings.

MULTIGRAIN BUTTERMILK ROLLS

- 1 cup quick-cooking oats
- ³/₄ cup buttermilk (see Note)
- ¹/₂ cup warm (105° to 115°) water
- 2 tablespoons sugar
- 1 envelope active dry yeast
- 2 cups all-purpose flour
- 1 cup whole-wheat flour
- 1¹/₄ teaspoons salt
- 3 tablespoons butter, melted
- 2 tablespoons molasses
  Melted butter, for brushing
  Oats, sesame seeds, or poppy seeds, for sprinkling (optional)

1. Place oats and buttermilk in 12-cup food processor. Let stand for 10 minutes.

2. Combine warm water, 1 teaspoon sugar, and yeast in small bowl. Let stand until foamy, about 5 minutes.

3. Add flours, remaining sugar, salt, and butter to processor. Add molasses to yeast mixture. With machine running,

*W*arm right out of the oven or cooled to room temperature, this upside-down cake is a treat all by itself. (Opposite) *From the cookie-crumb crust to the chocolate-covered espresso beans on top, cappuccino pie is pure delight.*

slowly add yeast mixture. When ball forms, process 1 minute. (If dough doesn't clear sides, add all-purpose flour, 2 tablespoons at a time. If too dry, add water, 1 tablespoon at a time.)

4. Place dough in large greased bowl; turn to coat. Cover loosely with plastic wrap. Let rise in warm place until doubled, about 1½ hours.

5. Punch dough down. Divide in half. Roll each half into 10-inch length. Cut each into 10 equal pieces. Shape into rolls. Place on greased baking sheet. Brush with melted butter. Cover with plastic wrap. Let rise at room temperature for 30 minutes. Refrigerate for 6 hours or overnight.

6. Heat oven to 375°. (If you wish, sprinkle rolls with oats, sesame seeds, or poppy seeds.)

7. Bake in 375° oven 20 minutes or until golden and hollow sounding when tapped. Cool on wire rack. Serve warm or at room temperature.

Note: For buttermilk, substitute 2 tablespoons dry buttermilk powder mixed in ¾ cup water.

Yield: Makes 20 rolls.

HOLIDAY UPSIDE-DOWN CAKE

Topping:

6	tablespoons (¾ stick) unsalted butter
½	cup firmly packed dark-brown sugar
1	can (16 ounces) pear halves in light syrup, drained and halved lengthwise
1	cup fresh or frozen cranberries

Cake:

1½	cups all-purpose flour
¾	cup granulated sugar
2	teaspoons baking powder
½	teaspoon salt
⅔	cup milk
⅓	cup unsalted butter, at room temperature
1	egg
2	teaspoons grated lemon zest
1	teaspoon vanilla

1. Heat oven to 350°.

2. Prepare Topping: Place butter in 9 x 9 x 2-inch-square baking pan. Place pan with butter in oven until butter melts. With pot holder, carefully remove the hot pan from oven. Stir in the brown sugar until well blended. Arrange the pear halves, rounded side down, decoratively over the sugar mixture in the buttered pan. Sprinkle cranberries between pears.

3. Prepare Cake: Stir together flour, sugar, baking powder, and salt in large bowl until well blended. Beat in milk and butter until smooth. Beat in egg, lemon zest, and vanilla until blended. Pour the batter evenly over the pears in baking pan.

4. Bake in 350° oven for 35 to 40 minutes or until a wooden pick inserted in the center of the cake comes out clean. Cool the cake in the pan on a wire rack for 5 minutes. With a small knife, loosen the sides of the cake from the pan. Place a serving platter on top of the pan; invert both the pan and the platter, letting the glaze drip down the sides of the cake. Remove the pan. Serve the upside-down cake warm or at room temperature.

Yield: Makes 16 servings.

CAPPUCCINO MOUSSE PIE

Crust:

- 1½ cups chocolate cookie crumbs (about 30 chocolate wafers, crumbled)
- ¼ cup sugar
- 6 tablespoons (¾ stick) butter, melted

Filling:

- ¾ cup double-strength brewed coffee, cooled
- 1 envelope unflavored gelatin
- 1 teaspoon instant espresso powder OR 2 teaspoons instant coffee powder
- ½ cup sugar
- 2 egg yolks
- ⅓ cup coffee liqueur
- ¼ cup egg-white powder (see Note)
- ¼ cup cold water
- 1½ cups heavy cream
  Chocolate-covered espresso beans and unsweetened cocoa powder, for garnish

1. Heat oven to 350°. Coat decorative 9-inch pie plate with nonstick vegetable-oil cooking spray.
2. Prepare Crust: Combine crumbs and sugar in small bowl. Stir in melted butter until blended. Scrape into pie plate; pat in even layer over bottom and up sides of plate.
3. Bake in 350° oven for 7 minutes. Transfer to wire rack to cool.
4. Prepare Filling: Combine ¼ cup of the coffee and gelatin in small bowl to soften, about 5 minutes.
5. Heat remaining coffee, espresso powder, and sugar in saucepan to bare simmer; stir in gelatin mixture to dissolve. Remove from heat. Whisk in yolks. Cook over low heat just until thickened; do not let boil.
6. Remove from heat. Stir in liqueur. Cool over ice water, stirring occasionally, until consistency of raw egg whites.
7. Meanwhile, beat egg-white powder and water in small bowl until peaks form. Beat cream in second bowl until stiff peaks form.
8. Fold beaten egg-white mixture into coffee mixture. Fold in 1 cup whipped cream; reserve remaining whipped cream for garnish. Scrape egg-white mixture into pie plate, spreading evenly. Chill at least 3 hours or overnight.
9. To serve, garnish with remaining whipped cream and espresso beans. Dust with cocoa powder.

Note: Egg-white powder is available in select supermarkets, gourmet shops, and health-food stores.

Yield: Makes 8 servings.

CHICORY SALAD

Salad:
- 1 small head (³/₄ pound) chicory
- 1 head (1 pound) red-leaf lettuce
- 1 bunch radishes, thinly sliced

Dressing:
- ¹/₃ cup olive oil
- ¹/₄ cup red-wine vinegar
- ¹/₄ cup rice-wine vinegar OR white-wine vinegar
- 2 teaspoons Dijon-style mustard
- 2 shallots OR white part of 2 green onions, chopped
- ¹/₄ cup finely chopped fresh parsley leaves
- ³/₄ teaspoon salt
- ¹/₄ teaspoon ground black pepper
- ¹/₄ teaspoon sugar

Croutons:
- 3 ounces fresh goat cheese OR fromage blanc
- 24 melba toast rounds (2¹/₄ ounces)
- ¹/₂ cup toasted walnuts, chopped

1. Prepare Salad: Rinse and dry chicory and lettuce. Cut chicory into 1-inch pieces. Tear red-leaf lettuce into pieces. Toss in large shallow serving bowl. Arrange radishes on top. Refrigerate, covered, for up to 1 day.
2. Prepare Dressing: Combine oil, vinegars, mustard, shallots, parsley, salt, pepper, and sugar in a jar with a tight-fitting lid; shake. (Can be prepared up to 2 days ahead and refrigerated. Shake before using.)
3. Prepare Croutons: Spread goat cheese on toast up to 4 hours in advance. Sprinkle with ¹/₄ cup walnuts. Add remaining walnuts to dressing.
4. To serve, arrange croutons around outer edge of salad. Serve with dressing.
Yield: Makes 20 servings.

Earthy seasonings from the south of France promise a mouth-watering meal: (This page, from top) Serve a salad of fresh chicory after the entrée, as the French do; surround with meltingly good croutons topped with goat cheese and walnuts. Entice the palate with a pungent spread of pesto and roasted peppers.

PESTO-RED PEPPER CREAM SPREAD

- 3 packages (8 ounces each) reduced-fat cream cheese (Neufchâtel), at room temperature
- 2 cups packed fresh basil leaves
- ¹/₄ cup pine nuts
- 2 cloves garlic, coarsely chopped
- ¹/₄ cup grated Parmesan cheese
- 1 jar (7 ounces) roasted red peppers, drained
- 2 teaspoons cornstarch
- ¹/₂ cup finely chopped green onions
  Fresh basil leaves and tomato rose, for garnish (optional)
  Thin slices of party bread, crackers, or pita chips

1. Beat cream cheese in large bowl until light and fluffy. Divide into thirds.
2. For pesto, combine basil, pine nuts, and garlic in food processor. Whirl until finely chopped.
3. Stir basil mixture into one third of the cream cheese, along with Parmesan cheese, until well blended.
4. Place red peppers in clean food processor bowl. Whirl until puréed. Transfer to small skillet. Whisk in cornstarch until well blended and smooth. Bring to simmering over medium heat; cook for about 3 to 5 minutes or until thickened. Cool for 15 minutes. Whisk into another third of cream cheese until well blended.
5. Mix green onion into the remaining third of cream cheese until blended.
6. Line 6-cup bowl with plastic wrap, leaving 2-inch overhang.
7. Turn pesto into lined bowl; pack firmly. Spoon on green onion mixture; carefully spread to cover pesto layer. Top with red pepper layer, spreading to completely cover onion layer. Cover the top with the plastic wrap overhang. Refrigerate for 2 to 3 hours or until firm.
8. Fold back the plastic wrap; unmold onto serving plate. Garnish with fresh basil leaves and tomato rose, if desired. Serve with bread, crackers, or pita chips.
Yield: Makes 5 cups.

CASSIS-GLAZED BAKED HAM

12-pound cured ham, rinsed
Cassis Glaze (recipe follows)

1. Bake ham on rack in roasting pan in preheated 350° oven for 3 hours (about 15 minutes per pound) or until internal temperature registers 140° on instant-read meat thermometer.
2. Brush with Cassis Glaze. Return to oven and bake 10 minutes. Let stand 10 minutes before slicing.
Yield: Makes 16 servings plus leftovers.

CASSIS GLAZE

Glaze can be prepared up to a week ahead and refrigerated.

- 1 tablespoon olive oil
- 1 small onion, chopped
- 2 large cloves garlic, chopped
- 1 cup cassis (black currant) liqueur OR cranberry juice
- ½ cup no-salt-added tomato sauce
- 1 tablespoon red-wine vinegar
- 1 tablespoon chopped fresh rosemary
- ½ teaspoon salt
- ¼ teaspoon crushed red-pepper flakes

Heat oil in saucepan over medium heat. Add onion and garlic; cook 4 minutes or until softened. Add cassis, tomato sauce, vinegar, rosemary, salt, and red-pepper flakes. Simmer 20 minutes, stirring, or until reduced to about 1 cup.
Yield: Makes about 1 cup.

ROASTED POTATOES WITH GARLIC AND ROSEMARY

- 16 red potatoes (about 3 pounds)
- 2 large cloves garlic, slivered
- 1 large sprig fresh rosemary, stem removed
- ½ teaspoon salt
- ¼ teaspoon ground black pepper
- 2 tablespoons olive oil (optional)

1. Cook potatoes in boiling water for 10 minutes or until just tender. Drain and cool.

2. Slice potatoes about two-thirds of the way through. Insert sliver of garlic and about 4 leaves of rosemary sprig into slices. Thread potatoes on skewers.
3. Bake the potatoes directly on oven rack in preheated 350° oven for 25 to 30 minutes or until they are heated through. Arrange on platter. Sprinkle with salt and pepper and drizzle with olive oil, if you wish.
Yield: Makes 12 servings.

The star of the show is a ham brushed with piquant black-currant glaze. Slip fresh herbs into potatoes; roast on skewers.

STRING BEANS PROVENÇAL

- 1 tablespoon olive oil
- 4 medium-size onions, chopped (2 cups)
- 4 cloves garlic, chopped
- 1 can (28 ounces) plum tomatoes in thick purée
- 2 teaspoons dried leaf thyme, crumbled
- 2 teaspoons sugar
- 1/4 teaspoon salt
- 1/4 teaspoon ground black pepper
- 2 pounds string beans, trimmed and halved

Heat oil in Dutch oven over medium heat. Add onions and garlic; cook, covered, stirring occasionally, 8 minutes or until softened. Add tomatoes, thyme, sugar, salt, and pepper, breaking up tomatoes with back of spoon. Stir in string beans. Simmer, covered, stirring occasionally, 25 to 30 minutes or until beans are tender. (Can be made a day ahead and refrigerated.) Serve the dish hot or warm.

Yield: Makes 12 servings.

Complement the meal with herbed vegetables: (From left) Onions, tomato, and thyme enrich string beans; Parmesan and capers season golden baked cauliflower. A colorful tian layers zucchini, eggplant, and red peppers.

CAULIFLOWER GRATIN

- 10 cups water
- 1 cup milk
- 2 teaspoons salt
- 2 heads cauliflower (2 1/2 pounds each), cut into flowerets
- 3 tablespoons olive oil
- 1 tablespoon fresh lemon juice
- 1 1/2 teaspoons drained capers
- 1 teaspoon anchovy paste
- 1/2 teaspoon Dijon-style mustard
- 1/4 cup fresh bread crumbs
- 1/4 cup grated Parmesan cheese

1. Bring water, milk, and salt to boiling in large saucepan. Working in batches if necessary, add cauliflower; simmer about 4 minutes or until tender-crisp. Drain; rinse the cauliflower under cold running water to stop the cooking.
2. Coat jelly-roll pan with nonstick vegetable-oil cooking spray. Arrange cauliflower in single layer on pan. Combine oil, lemon juice, capers, anchovy paste, and mustard in blender. Whirl until smooth. Drizzle evenly over cauliflower. Sprinkle on bread crumbs and Parmesan cheese. (Can be prepared a day ahead and refrigerated.)
3. Bake on upper rack of preheated 350° oven for 45 minutes or until crisped and thoroughly heated through. Serve hot or warm.

Yield: Makes 12 servings.

VEGETABLE TIAN

- 1 leek, trimmed, quartered lengthwise, and rinsed well
- 1 1/2 teaspoons dried leaf basil, crumbled
- 3 zucchini (1 1/2 pounds), trimmed
- 2 Japanese eggplant (14 ounces), peeled, OR 2 yellow squash
- 2 large sweet red peppers
- 3 tablespoons olive oil
- 1 teaspoon dried leaf thyme, crumbled
- 1/4 teaspoon crushed red-pepper flakes
- 1/2 teaspoon salt

1. Thinly slice leek. Scatter in a 15 x 10-inch ovenproof oval casserole or 13 x 9 x 2-inch baking dish. Sprinkle on the basil.
2. Diagonally slice zucchini and eggplant about 1/4 inch thick. Cut red peppers into 1-inch pieces. Arrange vegetables in casserole in overlapping rows.
3. Heat oil in small skillet over medium heat until fragrant. Remove from heat. Add thyme, red-pepper flakes, and salt. Let stand 20 minutes or until cooled slightly. Brush evenly over vegetables. (Can be refrigerated for up to 24 hours.)
4. Bake in preheated 350° oven on upper rack for 60 to 75 minutes or until vegetables are fork-tender. (Can be made up to 4 hours in advance.) Serve warm or at room temperature.

Yield: Makes 12 servings.

5. Divide mixture into three equal portions. Add green food coloring to one portion and red food coloring to another, leaving the last portion yellow. Separately spread each colored portion into prepared pans.

6. Bake in 350° oven 15 minutes or until edges are golden brown. Immediately remove the cakes from the pans, using the waxed paper overhang.

7. Heat apricot preserves in small saucepan; strain through sieve. Place the green cake layer on a jelly-roll pan. Spread half of warm preserves over this layer to the edges; slide the yellow layer on top; spread with remaining apricot preserves; slide the pink layer, right side up, onto the yellow layer.

8. Cover with plastic wrap; weight with large wooden cutting board or heavy plate. Place in refrigerator overnight.

9. Melt chocolate in double boiler over hot water. Trim edges off cake. Spread melted chocolate to edges of cake; let dry 10 minutes or until hardened. Cut into 1-inch squares.

Yield: Makes about 6 dozen squares.

For a delightful sweet that's not too heavy, sandwich apricot jam between almond-flavored layers of pink, yellow, and green cake. Top the Venetians with rich chocolate and arrange prettily on your best cake stand.

HOLIDAY VENETIANS

1	can (8 ounces) almond paste
1½	cups (3 sticks) butter, softened
1	cup sugar
4	eggs, separated
1	teaspoon almond extract
2	cups sifted all-purpose flour
¼	teaspoon salt
10	drops liquid green food coloring
8	drops liquid red food coloring
1	jar (12 ounces) apricot preserves
2½	squares (1 ounce each) semisweet chocolate

1. Heat oven to 350°. Coat three 13 x 9 x 2-inch baking pans with nonstick vegetable-oil cooking spray; line with waxed paper, allowing paper to come up the short ends; spray paper.

2. Break up almond paste in large bowl. Add butter, sugar, egg yolks, and almond extract. Beat with electric mixer until light and fluffy, about 5 minutes.

3. Beat in flour and salt.

4. Beat egg whites in a small bowl with electric mixer until stiff peaks form. Fold into almond mixture until well blended.

it's party time!

SAVORY MORSELS GUESTS CAN NIBBLE THE
MINUTE THEY WALK IN THE DOOR HELP MAKE ANY
PARTY A SMASH HIT. ELEGANT AND EASY, THESE
TASTY BITES ARE MOSTLY DO-AHEADS YOU
SERVE AT THE PEAK MOMENT.

FENNEL AND OLIVE TURNOVERS

Parsley Pastry:

- 1 teaspoon active dry yeast
- 1 teaspoon sugar
- 1/3 cup warm milk (115°)
- 1/2 cup (1 stick) butter, melted and cooled
- 3/4 cup chopped fresh parsley leaves
- 1 egg
- 1/2 teaspoon salt
- 2 1/4 cups all-purpose flour

Filling:

- 1 tablespoon olive oil
- 1 large onion, coarsely chopped
- 1 pound fennel bulbs, trimmed and coarsely chopped (3 cups)
- 1 teaspoon dried leaf rosemary, crumbled
- 1/2 teaspoon salt
- 1/4 teaspoon ground black pepper
- 1/4 cup pitted oil-cured black olives, finely chopped

1. Prepare Pastry: Sprinkle yeast over sugar and warm milk in large bowl. Let stand 5 minutes until foamy. Stir in butter, parsley, egg, and salt. Gradually stir in flour until smooth, soft dough forms. Knead gently in bowl 2 minutes. Cover; let stand 10 minutes.
2. Prepare Filling: Heat oil in large nonstick skillet over medium heat. Add onion; sauté 3 minutes. Add fennel; sauté 5 minutes. Add rosemary, salt, and pepper. Reduce heat to very low. Cover; cook, stirring occasionally, 20 minutes. Remove from heat. Stir in olives. Cool slightly.
3. Heat oven to 350°. Roll out pastry to 1/16-inch thickness. With 4-inch biscuit cutter, cut out 24 circles. Place scant measuring tablespoon filling in center of each. Moisten edge of pastry with water. Fold over; crimp and seal with tines of fork. Place on ungreased baking sheet.
4. Bake in 350° oven for 20 to 25 minutes or until pastry is golden. Cool. Serve at room temperature.
Yield: Makes 2 dozen.

ENDIVE WITH SMOKED SALMON

- 1 container (8 ounces) low-fat (1%) cottage cheese
- 4 ounces Neufchâtel cheese
- 4 ounces sliced smoked salmon
- 1 tablespoon chopped fresh dill
- 1/8 teaspoon ground black pepper
- 6 drops liquid red-pepper seasoning
- 2 large heads Belgian endive
  Red caviar, capers, dill sprigs, or watercress sprigs, for garnish (optional)

1. Combine cottage cheese and Neufchâtel in food processor. Whirl until smooth, about 1 minute.
2. Add salmon, dill, black pepper, and red-pepper seasoning. Whirl to mix. Refrigerate until ready to use.
3. Separate endive into leaves. Pipe or spoon 1 tablespoon cheese mixture into each of 24 leaves. Garnish, if you wish, with caviar, capers, dill, or watercress.
Yield: Makes 1 1/2 cups filling.

SHRIMP AND TORTELLINI PICKUPS

- 1 pound frozen tricolor cheese tortellini
- 1 pound large shrimp, shelled and deveined
- 1 sweet red pepper, cut into 1-inch squares
- 2 jars (6 ounces each) marinated artichoke hearts
- 2 tablespoons Dijon-style mustard
- 1/2 teaspoon ground black pepper

1. Cook tortellini following package directions, omitting salt. Add shrimp and red pepper for last 2 minutes of cooking.
2. Meanwhile, combine artichoke hearts with their marinade, mustard, and black pepper in large bowl. Drain tortellini mixture in large colander. Rinse with cold water to stop cooking; drain well. Add to artichoke mixture. Refrigerate up to 6 hours. Toss before serving.
3. To serve, skewer shrimp, artichoke, and red pepper pieces on wooden picks.
Yield: Makes 16 servings.

BROCCOLI-CHEDDAR DIP

- 1 container (8 ounces) low-fat (1%) cottage cheese
- 1 cup cubed white Cheddar cheese
- 1 package (10 ounces) frozen chopped broccoli, thawed and drained
- 1 green onion, trimmed and sliced
- 1/4 teaspoon salt
- 1/8 teaspoon ground black pepper
  Pinch of ground nutmeg
- 1/4 cup plain low-fat yogurt
  Chopped fresh chives, for garnish (optional)

1. Combine cottage cheese and Cheddar in food processor. Whirl until almost smooth, about 3 minutes.
2. Add broccoli, onion, salt, pepper, and nutmeg. Whirl to mix. Add yogurt. Pulse just to combine. Turn into serving bowl.
3. Garnish with chives, if you wish. Refrigerate, covered.
Yield: Makes about 2 3/4 cups.

RED PEPPER-CREAM CHEESE DIP WITH CRUDITÉS

- 1 container (8 ounces) low-fat (1%) cottage cheese
- 4 ounces Neufchâtel cheese
- 1 jar (7 ounces) roasted red peppers, drained and rinsed
- 1/4 teaspoon liquid red-pepper seasoning
- 1/2 cup low-fat plain yogurt

1. Combine cottage cheese and Neufchâtel in food processor. Whirl until almost smooth, 2 minutes.

For the Midas touch, scatter golden caviar over Endive with Smoked Salmon (opposite, from left). A mustardy marinade enlivens Shrimp and Tortellini Pickups. Even dieters can indulge in low-fat Broccoli-Cheddar Dip and Red Pepper-Cream Cheese Dip with Crudités.

2. Add half the red peppers and red-pepper seasoning. Whirl mixture until almost blended.

3. Coarsely chop remaining peppers. Add yogurt and peppers to processor. Pulse just to combine. Refrigerate, covered. To serve, top with additional chopped red peppers, if you wish.
Yield: Makes about 2$\frac{1}{4}$ cups.

VEGETABLE CRUDITÉS
Curry Dip:
- 1 cup reduced-fat mayonnaise
- 1 cup reduced-fat sour cream
- 1 teaspoon curry powder
- 2 tablespoons prepared plum sauce
- $\frac{1}{4}$ cup chopped fresh parsley leaves
- $\frac{1}{2}$ teaspoon ground black pepper
- $\frac{1}{4}$ teaspoon salt

Roasted Pepper Dip:
- 1 jar (7 ounces) roasted red peppers, drained and chopped
- 2 teaspoons dried leaf basil
- $\frac{1}{2}$ teaspoon salt
- $\frac{1}{2}$ teaspoon ground black pepper
- 1 cup reduced-fat sour cream
- 1 cup reduced-fat mayonnaise
- 2 tablespoons grated Parmesan cheese

Vegetables:
- 4 carrots, peeled, cut into sticks
- 2 sweet red peppers, cored, seeded, and sliced into strips
- 1 head broccoli, trimmed and cut into flowerets with stems
- 2 zucchini, cut into sticks

Combine ingredients for Curry Dip and then for Roasted Pepper Dip. Serve dips with vegetables.
Yield: Makes 16 servings.

Two tempting dips — curry mayo and roasted red pepper — put a zingy spin on the crudité tray. Whip up the dips the night before, and choose vegetables in a mix of scrumptious colors and textures.

EVERGREEN BREADSTICKS

- ¼ cup grated Parmesan cheese
- 3 tablespoons chopped fresh rosemary
- 2 teaspoons chopped fresh thyme OR 1 teaspoon dried leaf thyme, crumbled
- 1 teaspoon ground black pepper
- 1 sheet frozen puff pastry (half of 17¼-ounce package), thawed according to package directions

1. Heat oven to 400°.
2. Combine Parmesan, rosemary, thyme, and pepper in small bowl.
3. Unfold pastry on lightly floured surface. Sprinkle evenly with cheese mixture. Roll out with lightly floured rolling pin into 15 x 10-inch rectangle. Scrape any cheese sticking to rolling pin back onto pastry; press into pastry.
4. Cut pastry crosswise into ½-inch-wide strips. Twist each strip to form spiral stick. Place on ungreased baking sheet.
5. Bake in 400° oven 8 to 10 minutes or until golden brown. Transfer breadsticks to a wire rack to cool.
Yield: Makes about 30 sticks.

CARAMEL EGGNOG

- 1 cup granulated sugar
- 2 tablespoons plus ¼ cup water
- ½ teaspoon fresh lemon juice
- 6 eggs
- 4 cups low-fat milk (1%)
- ½ teaspoon vanilla
- ⅛ teaspoon grated nutmeg
- ⅛ teaspoon salt
- ¾ cup heavy cream
- 1 tablespoon confectioners' sugar Grated nutmeg and sliced almonds, for garnish (optional)

1. Combine sugar, 2 tablespoons water, and lemon juice in saucepan. Boil over medium heat 5 minutes or until dark amber. Turn off heat and carefully add ¼ cup water; it may splatter. Stir to dissolve caramel.
2. Whisk eggs and milk in bowl. Stir into caramel mixture. Cook over

medium-low heat 12 to 15 minutes until thickened enough to coat spoon (160° on instant-read thermometer). Immediately strain into clean bowl. Stir in vanilla, nutmeg, and salt. Refrigerate, covered, until chilled.
3. To serve: Beat together cream and confectioners' sugar in small bowl until soft peaks form. Pour egg mixture into serving bowl. Fold in whipped cream. Garnish with nutmeg and almonds, if desired.
Yield: Makes 10 servings.

Crispy herbed Evergreen Breadsticks (above) are great to crunch on. A hint of caramel adds sweetness to this eggnog (left), so rich it doesn't need any spirits.

SONORA CHEESE DIP

2 cups shredded Monterey Jack
    cheese (8 ounces)
2 cups shredded American cheese
    (8 ounces)
6 green onions, sliced
$^2/_3$ cup finely chopped sweet
    red pepper
2 tablespoons finely chopped,
    seeded jalapeño pepper

Melt together Monterey Jack and
American cheeses in top of double boiler
over simmering water, 5 to 10 minutes.
Stir in green onion, red pepper, and
jalapeño pepper. Serve hot with
tortilla chips.
Yield: Makes about 2 cups.

*A peppery blend of
Monterey Jack and American
cheeses, Sonora Cheese Dip
(above, from left) is a zesty
winner with tortilla chips. The
garlic-herb purée of sweet
potato and butternut squash
is pleasing on toasted
French bread or cucumber
rounds or stuffed into celery.
(Opposite) Varied toppings —
olives, green onion, sun-dried
tomatoes, and jalapeño peppers
— make quick pizza a finger-
food favorite.*

TOASTED FRENCH BREAD WITH WINTER VEGETABLE SPREAD

1 small sweet potato (6 ounces)
1 small butternut squash
    ($1^1/_2$ pounds), halved
    lengthwise and seeded
8 to 10 cloves garlic, unpeeled
1 tablespoon olive oil
1 teaspoon leaf marjoram, crumbled
$^3/_4$ teaspoon salt
$^1/_2$ teaspoon leaf thyme, crumbled
1 long loaf French bread, cut into
    32 thin slices

1. Heat oven to 400°. Lightly coat a
shallow baking dish with nonstick
vegetable-oil cooking spray. Place potato
and squash, cut side down, in dish.
2. Bake for 45 minutes or until squash
and potato are very tender. Add
unpeeled garlic cloves for last
20 minutes of baking time.
3. Scoop flesh from squash and potato
into food processor. Whirl until almost
smooth. Squeeze garlic cloves from
papery skin into processor. Add oil,
marjoram, salt, and thyme. Whirl to
combine. Refrigerate, covered, until
ready to use.
4. Toast bread slices in single layer
on baking sheets in 400° oven 6 to
8 minutes, turning slices once, until
lightly toasted. Cool completely. Store
in airtight container. To serve, spread
1 tablespoon purée on each slice toast.
Yield: Makes $1^3/_4$ cups.

TASTY PIZZA SQUARES

$1^1/_2$ tablespoons dry-pack sun-dried
    tomatoes
1 tube (10 ounces) refrigerated
    pizza dough
$^1/_2$ cup bottled marinara sauce
    OR pizza sauce
$^1/_3$ cup bottled pesto sauce
$1^1/_2$ cups shredded mozzarella cheese
    (6 ounces)
$^1/_4$ cup sliced canned black olives
$^1/_4$ cup sliced green onions
1 to 2 tablespoons chopped
    jalapeño pepper

1. Heat oven to 425°. Grease a
$15^1/_2$ x $10^1/_2$-inch baking pan.
2. Meanwhile, soak sun-dried tomatoes
in very hot water to cover in a bowl
until softened, about 5 minutes. Drain.
Chop.
3. Roll dough onto prepared baking pan.
Press dough to sides of pan.
4. Bake in 425° oven for 10 to
12 minutes or until golden brown.
5. Top half the dough with red sauce
and other half with pesto sauce. Top
with mozzarella cheese, olives, green
onion, sun-dried tomatoes, and jalapeño
pepper.
6. Bake in 425° oven for 5 to
10 minutes or until cheese melts.
Cut into 15 squares.
Yield: Makes 15 squares.

The perfect bite: a mushroom cap filled with peppers, bacon, and Cheddar cheese (clockwise from left). Pear wedges stuffed with blue cheese and wrapped with honey-baked ham are totally simple, totally delicious. Chicken crusted with coconut and peanuts tastes sublime with honey-orange sauce. Pretty pink Port-wine cream cheese is luscious on an endive leaf.

CHILI-MUSHROOM CAPS

 4 slices bacon
24 medium-size mushrooms
    (1 1/2 pounds)
 1 tablespoon butter
1/4 cup finely chopped onion
 1 clove garlic, finely chopped
1/3 cup finely chopped sweet red
    pepper
 2 to 3 pickled jalapeño peppers,
    seeded and finely chopped
1/2 cup shredded Cheddar cheese
1/4 cup chopped fresh parsley leaves

1. Cook bacon in skillet until almost crisp. Remove bacon from skillet; chop. Drain fat from skillet.
2. Remove stems from mushrooms. Finely chop two-thirds of stems. Save stems from remaining mushrooms for soup-making or other uses.
3. Cook mushroom caps in boiling water 1 minute. Drain; rinse under cold water. Drain on paper toweling.
4. Heat oven to 350°. Heat butter in skillet. Add chopped mushrooms, onion, and garlic; cook 5 minutes. Add red pepper and jalapeño; cook 3 minutes. Cool. Stir in bacon, cheese, and parsley. Spoon mixture into mushroom caps. Place on baking sheet.
5. Bake in 350° oven 10 minutes or until cheese is melted.
Yield: Makes 24 mushroom caps.

ENDIVE CUPS

 3 ounces Port-wine cheese, at
    room temperature
 2 ounces reduced-fat cream cheese,
    at room temperature
 3 heads Belgian endive
24 sprigs fresh parsley

1. Beat together Port-wine cheese and cream cheese in small bowl until creamy. Spoon mixture into pastry bag fitted with star tip.
2. Cut base from each head of endive; separate into leaves. Pipe small amount of cheese into base of each leaf. Refrigerate 15 minutes. Garnish each with parsley.
Yield: Makes about 24 "cups."

RASPBERRY CHAMPAGNE PUNCH

 2 packages (10 ounces each) frozen
    raspberries in light syrup,
    thawed
1 1/2 cups apricot nectar, chilled
 1 cup white grape juice, chilled
1/4 cup fresh lemon juice
 2 tablespoons honey
 1 bottle champagne OR sparkling
    white wine, chilled

1. Purée raspberries in blender or processor. Strain through sieve into punch bowl; discard seeds. Add nectar, grape juice, lemon juice, and honey to raspberries.
2. To serve: Stir champagne into raspberry mixture in punch bowl. Garnish with lemon, raspberries, and mint, if desired. (Can be prepared day ahead through Step 1; refrigerate, covered.)
Yield: Makes 12 servings.

PEAR WRAPS

 2 ripe pears
1/2 lemon
 3 ounces blue cheese, crumbled
1/4 pound thinly sliced honey-baked
    ham, cut into 1-inch-wide strips

Halve and core pears; cut each pear lengthwise into 8 equal wedges. Rub cut surface with lemon to prevent discoloration. Press a little cheese into cored cavity in each pear wedge.

Wrap each wedge in ham strip. Secure each with a wooden pick.
Yield: Makes 16 appetizers.

COCONUT-PEANUT CHICKEN

3/4 cup cocktail peanuts
 2 cups sweetened flaked coconut
1/4 cup all-purpose flour
 2 eggs
 1 pound boneless, skinned chicken
    breasts, cut into 1-inch pieces
    Vegetable oil, for cooking

Dipping Sauce:
 3 tablespoons honey
 3 tablespoons orange marmalade
 1 tablespoon soy sauce
1/2 teaspoon prepared mustard

1. Place peanuts in a food processor. Whirl until finely chopped. Combine the peanuts with coconut in a medium-size bowl. Place flour in a second bowl. Lightly beat the eggs in a third bowl.
2. Dip chicken pieces in flour to coat, then in egg, and then in peanut-coconut mixture.
3. Pour enough oil into electric skillet or regular large skillet to depth of 1/2 inch. Set electric skillet at 350° or heat oil in regular skillet over medium heat until oil registers 350° on deep-fat-frying thermometer. With slotted spoon, carefully add chicken to hot oil, 6 pieces at a time. Cook 4 to 6 minutes or until cooked through, turning once; adjust heat as needed to prevent peanut coating from overbrowning. Transfer chicken to paper toweling to drain. Repeat with remaining chicken.
4. Prepare Dipping Sauce: Combine honey, marmalade, soy sauce, and mustard in a small bowl. Serve with chicken.
Yield: Makes 30 servings.

Ruby-red Raspberry Champagne Punch (above) is fruity and fizzy.

grand finales

THE BEST PARTIES HAVE THE SWEETEST
ENDINGS — AND THESE DESSERTS PULL OUT
ALL THE STOPS. A FINAL FLOURISH OF FLAVOR,
PRESENTED IN SEASONAL STYLE, ELEVATES
EVEN THE MOST CASUAL CELEBRATION
INTO AN AFFAIR TO REMEMBER.

AMBROSIA CAKE

- 1 package (18.25 ounces) yellow cake mix
  Grated zest of 2 large oranges
- 1 cup orange juice
- 3 eggs
- 1 cup shredded coconut
- 1/4 cup golden rum
  Confectioners' sugar, whipped cream, strawberries, grapes, and edible flowers and leaves, for garnish (optional)

1. Place rack in lower third of oven. Heat oven to 325°. Grease and flour 10 x 4-inch fluted cake pan.
2. Combine cake mix, orange zest, orange juice, and eggs in large mixer bowl. Beat at low speed until combined, then beat at medium speed 3 minutes. Stir in shredded coconut. Pour batter into prepared pan.
3. Bake in 325° oven 55 to 65 minutes or until wooden pick inserted in center of cake comes out clean. Cool in pan on wire rack 15 minutes. Remove cake from pan. Transfer to cake plate. Poke holes in cake using fork with long tines. Slowly pour on rum. Cool to room temperature.
4. Cover cake securely. Store overnight to mellow.
5. Sift confectioners' sugar over cake. Garnish with whipped cream, strawberries, grapes, and edible flowers and leaves, if you wish.
Yield: Makes 16 servings.

*U*se shortcuts like box mixes to get a head-start on divine desserts. Ambrosia Cake is garnished with whipped cream and fruity flourishes (opposite). A mound of devil's food cake sprinkled with coconut, our Snowball Cake is not only simple — it's simply spectacular!

SNOWBALL CAKE

Cake:
- 1 package (18.25 ounces) devil's-food-cake mix
- 1 1/3 cups water
- 1/3 cup vegetable oil
- 3 eggs

Frosting:
- 1 1/2 cups sugar
- 1/2 cup water
- 3 tablespoons packaged meringue powder OR egg-white powder (see Note, page 84)
- 6 tablespoons water
- 1 cup shredded sweetened coconut
  Peppermint candies, for garnish (optional)

1. Place rack in lower third of oven. Heat oven to 325°. Grease and flour 2 1/2-quart ovenproof glass bowl.
2. Prepare Cake: Combine cake mix, water, oil, and eggs in large bowl. Beat at low speed until combined, then at medium speed 3 minutes. Pour batter into prepared bowl.
3. Bake in 325° oven for 1 hour 20 minutes or until wooden pick inserted in center of cake comes out clean. Cool cake in bowl on wire rack for 10 minutes. Invert cake onto rack; remove bowl. Cool cake completely.
4. Prepare Frosting: Combine sugar and the 1/2 cup water in medium-size saucepan. Bring to boil over medium-high heat; boil until syrup reaches soft-ball stage (240° on candy thermometer), about 15 minutes.
5. Meanwhile, mix meringue powder and the 6 tablespoons water in small bowl. Beat at medium speed until soft peaks form. Slowly add hot sugar syrup, beating at high speed until frosting cools and is very thick, about 5 minutes.
6. Assemble Snowball: Cut cake horizontally into thirds. Spread bottom layer with 3/4 cup frosting. Place middle layer on top; spread with 1/2 cup frosting. Put top layer in place; frost entire cake with remaining frosting. Gently pat coconut over all. Garnish base of cake with peppermint candies, if desired.
Yield: Make 12 servings.

MINCEMEAT TARTS

    1   cup currants
    ½   cup chopped dried apricots
    ½   cup raisins
    ⅓   cup chopped candied citron
    ⅓   cup chopped almonds
    1½ cups prepared applesauce
    ¼   cup brandy
    ¼   cup honey
    2   tablespoons fresh lemon juice
    ½   teaspoon ground cinnamon
    ½   teaspoon ground ginger
    ½   teaspoon grated nutmeg
    ¼   teaspoon ground allspice
    ¼   teaspoon salt
    2½ cups all-purpose flour
    ½   teaspoon salt
    6   tablespoons unsalted butter,
          chilled
    6   tablespoons vegetable shortening
    1   egg, beaten

1. Prepare mincemeat: Combine currants, apricots, raisins, citron, almonds, applesauce, brandy, honey, lemon juice, cinnamon, ginger, nutmeg, allspice, and salt in large saucepan. Bring to bare simmer and cook, covered, for 20 to 25 minutes or until fruit is softened and the mixture is thickened. Cool and refrigerate.

2. Prepare pastry: Combine flour and salt in large bowl. Cut in butter until mixture resembles fine meal. Add shortening and blend until mixture comes together. Flatten into a disk and chill at least 1 hour or up to 3 days.

3. Heat oven to 350°. Roll out dough to ⅜ inch thick. Cut out six 5-inch rounds. Use rounds to line six 4-inch tartlet shells. Prick pastry evenly with fork. Place on baking sheet and bake for 10 minutes. Fill each shell with ⅓ cup of the mincemeat, spreading level. Return to oven and bake 20 to 25 minutes or until pastry is golden. Remove and cool.

4. Cut 6 stars from remaining dough. Place stars on baking sheet and brush with beaten egg. Bake 5 to 7 minutes or until just beginning to color around edges. Place on wire rack to cool.

Topped with a celestial touch, Mincemeat Tarts (top) are filled with a luscious blend of fruits and spices. The fruit-plump Christmas Pudding is a Victorian treat. Cranberry-Nut Cheesecake (opposite) is a scrumptious show-off.

Arrange one cooled star on each cooled tart. Store refrigerated for up to 2 days. **Yield:** Make 6 servings.

CHRISTMAS PUDDING

    1   package (15 ounces) raisins
    1   package (10 ounces) dried
          currants
    2   containers (4 ounces each) diced
          candied citron OR candied fruit
    ½   cup brandy
    1   cup vegetable shortening
    1   cup firmly packed light-brown
          sugar
    ¼   cup honey
    4   eggs
    2½ cups all-purpose flour
    2   teaspoons salt
    2   teaspoons ground cinnamon
    1   teaspoon ground cloves
    1   teaspoon ground nutmeg
    1   teaspoon baking soda
        Plain dried bread crumbs

1. In large bowl, combine raisins, currants, and citron; sprinkle brandy over, and toss to coat. Let stand for 10 minutes.

2. In large bowl with electric mixer at high speed, beat shortening, brown sugar, and honey until creamy. Beat in eggs until fluffy.

3. In large bowl, stir flour, salt, cinnamon, cloves, nutmeg, and baking soda to blend. Add soaked fruits; stir until combined.

4. Grease 10-cup tube-type pudding mold; sprinkle with bread crumbs. Spoon batter into prepared mold. Cover with double thickness of aluminum foil; tie with string to secure.

5. Place on trivet in bottom of large, deep saucepot. Pour boiling water to half depth of mold; cover pot.

6. Bring water to simmer over low heat. At bare simmer, steam pudding, covered, adding more boiling water if needed, for 2 hours or until wooden skewer inserted in center comes out clean. Cool in mold on wire rack for 15 minutes. Loosen around edge of mold. Invert onto rack; cool completely. Wrap in plastic. Store for at least 2 weeks, refrigerated, to blend flavors; store frozen, wrapped in foil, for up to 2 months.

Note: To bake in oven, place batter in two 5-cup molds, greased and sprinkled with bread crumbs. Bake in preheated 325° oven for 1 hour or until skewer inserted in centers comes out clean.

Yield: Makes 16 servings.

CRANBERRY-NUT CHEESECAKE

Crust:

1/2	cup sifted all-purpose flour
1/4	teaspoon ground cinnamon
1/4	cup (1/2 stick) butter, chilled
1	teaspoon water
1/8	teaspoon vanilla
3/4	cup finely ground walnuts

Cheese Filling:

5	packages (8 ounces each) Neufchâtel cheese (low-fat cream cheese)
1 3/4	cups sugar
3	tablespoons all-purpose flour
12	ounces reduced-cholesterol liquid whole eggs
1	teaspoon grated lime zest
2	tablespoons fresh lime juice
1	teaspoon vanilla
	Cranberry Topping (recipe follows)

1. Heat oven to 400°.

2. Prepare Crust: Combine flour and cinnamon in medium size bowl. Cut in butter with pastry blender or 2 knives until mixture resembles coarse crumbs. Add water and vanilla; mix until dough holds together. Mix in 1/2 cup walnuts. (You can prepare crust in food processor: Grind 3/4 cup walnuts in processor. Remove and reserve 1/4 cup for topping. Add flour, cinnamon, butter, water, and vanilla. Pulse to combine.) Press crust mixture evenly with sheet of waxed paper into bottom of 9 x 3-inch springform pan.

3. Bake crust in 400° oven 10 minutes or until lightly golden. Cool on wire rack. Increase oven temperature to 475°.

4. Prepare Cheese Filling: Beat

Neufchâtel cheese in large bowl until smooth. Combine sugar and flour in small bowl. Gradually beat into cheese. Beat in liquid eggs. Stir in lime zest and juice and vanilla. (All the filling ingredients can be combined in a food processor and whirled together.)

5. Place springform pan on foil-lined jelly-roll pan. Pour in cheese mixture.

6. Bake in 475° oven 10 minutes. Reduce oven temperature to 200°. Bake 1 1/2 hours more. Remove cake from oven; run thin knife around edge of cake. Return cake to oven; let sit in oven with door ajar for 30 minutes. Transfer to wire rack to cool in pan completely. Cover and refrigerate until thoroughly chilled.

7. Remove sides of springform pan. Spread top of cheesecake with Cranberry Topping. Chill at least 30 minutes before serving for topping to set. Sprinkle top with remaining ground walnuts in a lattice pattern.

Cranberry Topping: Combine 2 cups fresh or frozen cranberries, 3/4 cup sugar, 1/4 teaspoon ground cinnamon, 1/8 teaspoon salt, and 2/3 cup water in saucepan. Bring to boiling over medium heat, stirring, until berries pop and mixture thickens, 8 to 10 minutes. Force mixture through strainer over bowl. Stir in 1 tablespoon fresh lime juice. Cool slightly before spreading on cheesecake.

Yield: Makes 16 servings.

PEACH CRUMBLE PIE

Crust:

- 4 ounces cream cheese, at room temperature
- 1/2 cup (1 stick) butter, at room temperature
- 1 cup all-purpose flour

Filling:

- 3 ounces dried peaches OR dried apricots, chopped
- 2 tablespoons peach nectar OR apple cider
- 1 bag (20 ounces) frozen peach slices, completely thawed
- 1/4 cup firmly packed brown sugar
- 1/4 cup all-purpose flour
- 1/4 cup (1/2 stick) butter, melted
- 2 tablespoons fresh lemon juice
- 1/2 teaspoon ground cinnamon

Topping:

- 1 cup all-purpose flour
- 1/2 cup finely chopped walnuts
- 1/2 cup firmly packed brown sugar
- 1/2 teaspoon ground cinnamon
  Pinch salt
- 6 tablespoons chilled butter, cut into small pieces
  Peach slices, for garnish (optional)

1. Prepare Crust: Beat cream cheese and butter in medium-size bowl on medium speed until smooth and creamy. On low speed, beat in flour until the mixture comes together. Pat dough into disk; wrap in plastic wrap; refrigerate 30 minutes.
2. Prepare Filling: Combine chopped dried peaches and peach nectar in medium-size saucepan. Simmer over medium-low heat for 10 minutes or until dried peaches are softened. Set aside to cool. Combine thawed peaches, sugar, flour, butter, lemon juice, and cinnamon in large bowl. Add cooled dried peaches. Set aside.
3. Heat oven to 450°.
4. Roll out dough into 12-inch circle. Fit into 9-inch pie pan. Fold excess dough under to form standup edge; flute edge. Refrigerate.
5. Prepare Topping: Combine the flour, walnuts, brown sugar, cinnamon, and salt in a medium-size bowl. Work in the butter with your fingertips until the mixture is crumbly and large pieces of butter are no longer visible. (Or chop the walnuts in a food processor. Add the flour, brown sugar, cinnamon, and salt; pulse with on-and-off motion to combine. Add the butter. Pulse until the mixture is crumbly.)
6. Spoon peach mixture into prepared pie shell. Sprinkle topping over all.
7. Bake pie on a baking sheet in 450° oven for 10 minutes. Lower oven temperature to 350°. Bake for 45 minutes or until filling is bubbly and topping is golden brown. Remove pie from oven to wire rack to cool slightly before serving. Garnish with peach slices, if you wish.
Yield: Makes 8 servings.

LIME CHIFFON PIE

Crust:

- 1 1/2 cups chocolate cookie crumbs
- 6 tablespoons unsalted butter, at room temperature
- 1/4 cup sugar

Filling:

- 1 package unflavored gelatin
- 1/4 cup cold water
- 4 egg yolks
- 1 cup sugar
- 2/3 cup Key lime or fresh lime juice
- 1 teaspoon grated lime zest
- 1/4 teaspoon salt
- 2 tablespoons plus 2 teaspoons meringue powder OR egg-white powder (see Note)
- 1/2 cup warm water
- 1 cup heavy cream
  Whipped cream, lime wedges, and Sugared Cranberries (recipe follows), for garnish (optional)

1. Heat oven to 375°.
2. Prepare Crust: Combine cookie crumbs, butter, and sugar in small bowl until blended. Press crumb mixture over bottom of 10-inch pie plate.
3. Bake in 375° oven for 6 minutes. Remove to wire rack to cool completely.
4. Prepare Filling: Sprinkle the unflavored gelatin over the cold water in a small bowl; let stand until the gelatin is softened, about 5 minutes.
5. Meanwhile, whisk together egg yolks and sugar in medium-size saucepan until well blended. Gradually mix in lime juice, lime zest, and salt. Cook over medium heat, stirring constantly, until the mixture thickens and coats the back of a spoon well; do not let boil or mixture will curdle. Remove from heat.
6. Stir softened gelatin mixture into the egg mixture until dissolved. Set aside to cool until slightly thickened.
7. Beat together the meringue powder and warm water in a medium-size bowl with mixer at high speed until soft peaks form. Fold cooled egg yolk mixture into meringue mixture until just blended.
8. Beat the heavy cream in a large bowl until stiff peaks form. Fold the meringue mixture gently into the whipped cream mixture until blended. Spoon the mixture into the cooled crust. Refrigerate until chilled, about 4 hours. Garnish with whipped cream, lime wedges, and sugared cranberries, if desired.
Sugared Cranberries: Melt 1/4 cup raspberry jam or other flavor in small saucepan. Add 1/2 cup cranberries; stir to coat. When cool enough to handle, roll each in granulated sugar.
Note: We prefer using meringue powder or egg-white powder when uncooked egg whites are usually called for, due to the increased concern about the presence of salmonella bacteria in raw eggs. Meringue powder and egg-white powder are available in stores where decorating and baking supplies are sold, and in some supermarkets.
Yield: Makes 10 servings.

Catch the spirit of the season with this trio (from top): Peach Crumble Pie lavished with crunchy walnuts, Lime Chiffon Pie fluted with whipped cream, and Black-and-White Cheesecake with feather-swirled top.

BLACK-AND-WHITE CHEESECAKE

- 1/4 cup vanilla wafer crumbs
- 4 packages (8 ounces each) cream cheese, at room temperature
- 16 ounces sour cream
- 1 cup sugar plus 2 tablespoons
- 1/2 cup (1 stick) butter, at room temperature
- 2 tablespoons cornstarch
- 2 teaspoons vanilla
- 5 eggs
- 4 squares (1 ounce each) semisweet chocolate, coarsely chopped
- 1/4 cup unsweetened cocoa powder, sifted

1. Heat oven to 350°. Grease 9-inch springform pan; sprinkle with cookie crumbs, tapping out any excess. Refrigerate while preparing the filling.
2. Beat together cream cheese, sour cream, the 1 cup sugar, butter, cornstarch, and vanilla in large bowl on low speed until mixed. Add the eggs, one at a time, beating after each addition just until combined. Do not overbeat.
3. Melt the chocolate in a small, heavy saucepan over lowest heat; stir in the remaining 2 tablespoons sugar. Remove 2 cups of batter to a clean bowl; stir in the melted chocolate and cocoa powder; the mixture will be thick.
4. Pour half of plain cheesecake batter into prepared pan. Spoon half of chocolate batter in dollops over top of plain batter. Repeat with remaining batters. Run knife through batter in figure-eight pattern to create a marble pattern.
5. Bake in 350° oven for 1 hour; center should still be soft. After first 30 minutes, loosely cover cheesecake with aluminum foil to prevent further browning. Turn oven off. Let cheesecake stand in oven, with door closed, for 1 hour. Remove pan to wire rack, away from drafts, to cool, about 4 hours. Remove sides of pan and refrigerate overnight.
Yield: Makes 16 servings.

EGGNOG MOCHA MUGS

- 2 1/2 cups prepared eggnog
- 1 envelope gelatin plus 1 teaspoon
- 2 tablespoons sugar
- 1/2 teaspoon rum extract
- 2 squares (1 ounce each) semisweet chocolate, coarsely chopped
- 2 teaspoons unsweetened cocoa powder, sifted
- 1 1/2 teaspoons instant coffee powder
- 1 teaspoon vanilla
- 1 cup heavy cream
  Cinnamon sticks, for garnish (optional)

1. Combine eggnog, gelatin, and sugar in small saucepan. Heat over medium heat until gelatin dissolves, stirring often. Remove 1 cup mixture to small bowl; stir in rum extract.
2. Add chocolate, cocoa, and coffee to mixture in saucepan. Cook over low heat, stirring, until chocolate melts. Add vanilla.
3. Chill mixtures separately until they mound when stirred; watch carefully and don't overchill or they will become lumpy.
4. Beat heavy cream in bowl until stiff peaks form. Fold one-third of whipped cream into plain eggnog mixture and the remaining two-thirds into chocolate mixture.
5. Spoon mixtures in layers in 4- to 5-ounce glasses or cups. Cover; refrigerate until set, about 2 hours.
Yield: Makes 8 servings.

TRADITIONAL YULETIDE LOG

- 10 eggs
- 1 cup all-purpose flour
- 1/4 teaspoon ground nutmeg
- 1 cup sugar
- 2 teaspoons vanilla
- 1 teaspoon rum extract
  Unsweetened cocoa powder
  Chocolate Cream Filling (recipe follows)
  Chocolate Ganache (recipe follows)

1. Separate eggs, placing yolks and whites into 2 separate large bowls. Let eggs come to room temperature for no more than 1 hour.
2. Heat oven to 350°. Grease two 15 1/2 x 10 1/2 x 1-inch jelly-roll pans. Line pans with waxed paper.
3. Combine flour and nutmeg on waxed paper.
4. Beat egg whites until frothy. Gradually beat in 1/2 cup sugar. Beat until stiff peaks form.
5. Beat yolks with remaining 1/2 cup sugar at high speed until thick and lemon-colored, about 5 minutes. Beat in vanilla and rum extract. Fold in flour.
6. Gently fold yolk mixture into whites until no white streaks remain. Divide between 2 prepared pans, spreading evenly.
7. Bake in 350° oven for 10 minutes or until cake springs back when gently pressed in center with fingertip.
8. Meanwhile, sprinkle cocoa powder over length of clean dish towel long enough to turn out both cakes onto. Turn out cakes onto cocoa-covered towel, slightly overlapping two long sides. Carefully peel off waxed paper. Beginning with a 15-inch side, roll up cakes with towel. Place, seam side down, on wire rack to cool.
9. Prepare Chocolate Cream Filling and Chocolate Ganache.
10. Unroll cake and towel. Spread cake evenly with Chocolate Cream Filling. Reroll cake without towel.
11. Cut each end from cake, using parallel diagonal cuts. Reserve ends to use as tree knots. Lift the cake, seam side

down, onto serving plate. Place a knot on each side of log, with diagonally cut side facing away from log. Spread ganache over log and knots, leaving all spiral ends exposed. For bark effect, run fork gently over frosting. Garnish with artificial greenery.

Chocolate Cream Filling: Pour 2 cups cold milk into bowl. Stir in two 3.9-ounce packages instant chocolate pudding-and-pie filling. Whisk until thickened, about 2 minutes. Fold in 1 cup whipped cream and 1 teaspoon vanilla.

Chocolate Ganache: Coarsely chop 6 ounces semisweet chocolate. Melt in bowl over hot, not simmering, water. Stir occasionally. Remove from heat. Pour 1 cup cream into chocolate, stirring with rubber spatula until smooth. Refrigerate, stirring occasionally, until spreading consistency, 20 to 30 minutes.
Yield: Makes 16 servings.

Chocolaty flavors and ready-to-use ingredients make Eggnog Mocha Mugs (opposite) a warming toast. Traditional Yuletide Log (below) is a showstopper — and simple to make with our step-by-step instructions. Hint: It all starts with two jelly-roll-style cakes.

TRUFFLE-TOPPED CHOCOLATE CAKE

    1 1/2 cups boiling water
     3/4   cup Dutch-processed
           unsweetened cocoa powder
      4   eggs
    1 1/2 teaspoons vanilla
    3 1/4 cups sifted cake flour
      2   cups sugar
      2   tablespoons baking powder
    1 1/2 teaspoons salt
      1   cup (2 sticks) unsalted butter

Fudge Frosting:

      1   pound semisweet chocolate
      2   cups heavy cream

Truffle Topping:

     1/2   cup heavy cream
      8   ounces bittersweet chocolate,
           chopped
      1   tablespoon unsalted butter
     1/2   teaspoon vanilla
      1   cup coarsely chopped walnuts
           Fresh raspberries, for garnish
           Confectioners' sugar

1. Heat oven to 350°. Grease three 9-inch round cake pans. Line with waxed-paper rounds; grease and flour waxed-paper rounds.

2. In bowl, whisk boiling water and cocoa until smooth. Cool to room temperature.

3. In small bowl, combine eggs with vanilla. Lightly whisk in one-quarter of cooled cocoa mixture.

4. In large bowl, combine flour, sugar, baking powder, and salt; beat with electric mixer at low speed for 1 minute or until blended.

5. Add remaining cocoa mixture and butter to flour mixture. Raise speed to medium-high; beat for 1 1/2 minutes, scraping down sides of bowl. Add egg mixture in thirds, beating at medium-high for 20 seconds after each addition. Pour batter into prepared pans.

6. Bake layers in 350° oven for 20 to 30 minutes or until wooden pick inserted near centers comes out clean. (Layers should not shrink from pan sides.) Cool layers in pans on wire racks

for 10 minutes. Loosen sides of layers and invert them onto lightly greased wire racks. Remove waxed paper.

7. Prepare Fudge Frosting: In food processor, chop chocolate very finely. Heat cream in saucepan until bubbles appear around edges. With motor running, add hot cream to chocolate in steady stream. Process until mixture is smooth. Transfer frosting to bowl. Let frosting cool at room temperature until good spreading consistency; do not stir frosting.

8. Prepare Truffle Topping: In small saucepan, heat cream until simmering. Remove from heat; stir in chocolate, butter, and vanilla. Stir until smooth; scrape into foil-lined 11 x 7-inch baking pan. Place topping in freezer until firm.

9. Spread frosting between 3 layers, sprinkling each layer with 1/4 cup chopped walnuts. Frost top and sides of cake. Cut chilled Truffle Topping into 3/4-inch cubes; scatter on top of cake. Garnish with raspberries and remaining chopped walnuts; sprinkle with confectioners' sugar.

Yield: Makes 12 servings.

DOBOS TORTE

      5   eggs, separated
     2/3   cup granulated sugar
      1   teaspoon vanilla
     2/3   cup sifted cake flour

Filling:

      4   squares (1 ounce each)
           unsweetened chocolate,
           coarsely chopped
      1   cup (2 sticks) unsalted butter
    2 1/2 to 3 cups sifted confectioners'
           sugar
     1/2   cup light cream or half-and-half
      1   tablespoon vanilla
           Lace Cookies (recipe, page 90)
           Brandy Cream (recipe, page 90)

1. Heat oven to 350°. Grease and line two 15 1/2 x 10 1/2 x 1-inch jelly-roll pans with waxed paper. Spray pans with nonstick vegetable-oil cooking spray.

2. In large bowl with electric mixer at high speed, beat egg whites until foamy.

Sprinkle in 1/3 cup of the granulated sugar, 1 tablespoon at a time, beating until meringue forms soft peaks.

3. In small bowl, beat egg yolks with remaining 1/3 cup granulated sugar and the 1 teaspoon vanilla until thick and fluffy; fold in flour. Stir in one-third of egg-white meringue; fold mixture into remaining meringue. Spread batter into prepared jelly-roll pans, dividing evenly; smooth tops of batter with spatula.

4. Bake in 350° oven for 12 minutes or until center springs back when lightly touched with fingertip. Invert onto wire racks or clean towels; peel off waxed paper; cool completely.

5. Cut each cake crosswise into 4 strips, each about 10 x 4 inches.

6. Prepare Filling: In top of double boiler, melt chocolate over hot, not boiling, water. Remove from heat; beat in butter until well blended. Beat in confectioners' sugar alternately with cream until filling is smooth and spreadable. Stir in vanilla.

7. Chill filling briefly, if too soft. Trim layers, if necessary, and stack (8 layers in all) on serving plate, spreading slightly rounded 1/4 cup filling between each layer. Smooth remaining filling on sides and top.

8. Prepare Lace Cookies: Arrange about 12 on top of torte. Pipe Brandy Cream into ends of cookies. Chill for several hours or overnight.

Yield: Makes 12 servings.

P*ure heaven: sinful Truffle-Topped Chocolate Cake (right) and eight-layer Dobos Torte with light-as-air Lace Cookies.*

LACE COOKIES

- 1/4 cup ground blanched almonds
- 1/4 cup sugar
- 1/4 cup (1/2 stick) unsalted butter
- 1 tablespoon all-purpose flour
- 1 tablespoon milk

1. Heat oven to 375°. In small saucepan, combine almonds, sugar, butter, flour, and milk. Heat, stirring constantly, just until butter is melted and mixture is smooth. Drop by teaspoonfuls, 4 inches apart, onto buttered and floured baking sheets. Work with only 4 or 5 cookies at a time.

2. Bake in 375° oven for 5 minutes or until cookies are lacy and golden brown. Cool briefly on baking sheets; working quickly, turn each cookie upside down with spatula, and quickly roll it around handle of wooden spoon. (If cookie cools too fast and is too brittle to work with, return it to warm oven for a few minutes.) Slide cookie off handle onto wire rack to cool.

Brandy Cream: In small bowl, beat 1/4 cup (1/2 stick) butter with 2/3 cup sifted confectioners' sugar and 2 teaspoons brandy until smooth. Fill Lace Cookies as directed in Step 8, page 88, of Dobos Torte.

Yield: Makes about 15 cookies.

No baking required! Molded in a mixing bowl, Cookie Tortoni Bombe (above) needs just six ingredients and an overnight stay in the freezer. This Jelly-Roll Trifle (opposite) puts a new spin on an old standard: sponge cake is spiraled with raspberry preserves to surround the sherried custard.

COOKIE TORTONI BOMBE

- 2 cups heavy cream
- 4 tablespoons sugar
- 1/2 teaspoon orange extract
- 1 package (6 ounces) mixed dried fruit bits OR 1 1/4 cups chopped mixed dried fruit
- 3 tablespoons orange marmalade
- 1 package (6 3/4 ounces) strawberry fruit cookies

1. Invert 6-cup slope-sided round bowl; press piece of aluminum foil over it to take shape of bowl. Turn bowl right side up; place foil shape inside to line bowl.

2. Combine 1 2/3 cups of the cream, 3 tablespoons of the sugar, and the orange extract in small electric-mixer bowl. Beat until soft peaks form. Fold in fruit bits and marmalade. Spoon into prepared bowl; spread level. Cover and freeze until completely frozen, about 4 hours.

3. Sometime before serving, combine the remaining 1/3 cup cream and remaining 1 tablespoon sugar in small bowl. Beat until stiff peaks form. Unmold bombe onto serving plate. Frost with whipped cream. Press cookies into cream, fruit side out, spacing evenly all around the outside. Cover and place in freezer until cream is firm. Cover bombe with plastic wrap; keep in freezer up to 3 weeks.

4. About half hour before serving, place bombe in refrigerator to soften slightly. Cut bombe into wedges with serrated knife.

Yield: Makes 10 servings.

JELLY-ROLL TRIFLE

Jelly Roll:

- 1 cup all-purpose flour
- 1 teaspoon baking powder
- 1/4 teaspoon salt
- 4 eggs
- 3/4 cup granulated sugar
- 1/4 cup orange juice
- 1 teaspoon vanilla
  Confectioners' sugar

Custard:

- 2/3 cup granulated sugar
- 1/4 cup cornstarch
- 1/4 teaspoon salt
- 4 cups milk
- 1/4 cup dry sherry
- 4 egg yolks
- 1/4 cup butter
- 1 tablespoon vanilla
- 3/4 cup seedless raspberry preserves
- 1 1/2 pints raspberries
- 1 cup heavy cream
- 2 tablespoons confectioners' sugar
- 1 teaspoon vanilla
- 1/2 cup sliced almonds, toasted

1. Heat oven to 375°. Grease 15^1/$_2$ x 10^1/$_2$-inch jelly-roll pan; line pan with waxed paper; grease paper.

2. Prepare Jelly Roll: Combine flour, baking powder, and salt in small bowl. Beat eggs in large bowl at medium speed until thickened slightly, about 2 minutes. Add sugar, 1 tablespoon at a time, beating until very thick and lemon colored, about 5 minutes. Beat in juice and vanilla. Beat in flour mixture until just mixed. Spread evenly in prepared pan.

3. Bake in 375° oven for 10 minutes or until top of cake springs back when lightly touched in center.

4. Sprinkle large towel with confectioners' sugar. When cake is done, immediately loosen edges and invert cake onto towel. Starting from short side, roll up cake, with towel, jelly-roll fashion. Cool cake, seam side down, on rack.

5. Prepare Custard: Mix sugar, cornstarch, and salt in saucepan. Gradually stir in milk and sherry. Bring to boil over medium heat, stirring constantly, until thickened. Boil 1 minute. Reduce heat to low.

6. Whisk yolks slightly in a small bowl. Beat in ^{1}/$_4$ cup hot milk mixture. Slowly pour yolk mixture back into milk mixture in saucepan over low heat, stirring quickly to prevent lumping. Heat, stirring, until custard thickens and thickly coats back of spoon.

7. Remove saucepan from heat. Stir in butter and vanilla. Transfer to a medium bowl. Cover surface with plastic wrap; refrigerate until well chilled, about 1 hour.

8. Unroll cooled cake. Spread with preserves. Roll up cake without towel. Cut in ^{1}/$_2$-inch-thick slices. Line sides of 14-cup glass bowl with half the slices. Cut remaining slices into quarters; layer alternately in center with custard and berries. Refrigerate, covered, 2 hours or overnight.

9. To serve, beat cream, confectioners' sugar, and vanilla in a bowl until soft peaks form. Spoon over top of trifle. Sprinkle with almonds.

Yield: Makes 12 servings.

F·U·N for all

LOOKING FOR HOLIDAY FUN FOR ALL? TRY THE
KITCHEN! THE KIDS CAN WHIP UP CANDIES AND
YUMMY GIFT BOXES EASY AS 1-2-3. THEY'LL WATCH
(AND CHEER!) AS YOU DECORATE WHIMSICAL
CAKES AND COOKIES FOR TABLE OR TREE.

Young chefs can make No-Bake Truffles in minutes: Roll our peanut-butter mixture between palms to form balls (hint: dust palms with confectioners' sugar first), dip each in chocolate, and roll in different toppings. Kids will love a happy Snowman Cake (opposite), covered in drifts of frosting and dressed with candies.

NO-BAKE TRUFFLES

- 1 cup smooth peanut butter
- 1/2 cup dark corn syrup
- 1 cup crisped-rice cereal
- 8 ounces milk chocolate, broken into pieces
- 1/4 cup finely chopped peanuts

1. Beat peanut butter and corn syrup in medium-size bowl until well blended. Stir in cereal until well mixed.
2. Line a large baking sheet with waxed paper. Shape teaspoonfuls of mixture into balls. Place on baking sheet. Refrigerate several hours or until firm.
3. In a medium-size bowl, melt chocolate in microwave for 1 minute on 50-percent power, stirring occasionally until smooth.
4. Using a fork, dip a peanut-butter ball in chocolate; remove excess chocolate. Roll truffle in chopped peanuts. Replace finished truffles on baking sheet. Refrigerate 1 hour or until firm. Try other coatings like coconut, colored sugars, nonpareils, or sprinkles on dark or white chocolate.
Yield: Makes 3 1/2 dozen.

SNOWMAN CAKE

- 2 1/2 cups all-purpose flour
- 1 teaspoon baking soda
- 3/4 teaspoon salt
- 1 cup buttermilk
- 1 tablespoon grated lemon zest
- 3 tablespoons fresh lemon juice
- 1/2 cup (1 stick) unsalted butter
- 1 1/2 cups granulated sugar
- 3 eggs
- 2 1/2 cups Buttercream Frosting (recipe follows)
  - Coarse sugar
  - 6 x 3-inch cardboard
  - Black paste food coloring

1. Heat oven to 325°. Grease and flour 4-inch, 5 1/2-inch, and 8-inch ovenproof mixing bowls. Set aside; use other bowls for Steps 2 and 3.

2. Mix flour, baking soda, and salt in bowl. In separate bowl, mix buttermilk, lemon zest, and juice.

3. In large third bowl, beat butter and granulated sugar. Beat in eggs, 1 at a time. Beat in flour alternately with buttermilk mixture. Pour into the 3 prepared bowls.

4. Bake in 325° oven 30 to 50 minutes, removing smallest cake after 30 minutes if toothpick tests clean. Cool 5 minutes. Run knife around edges to loosen; unmold cakes. Cool on racks completely.

5. Place 2 larger cakes next to each other. Spread with 2 cups frosting. Sprinkle with coarse sugar.

6. For hat, cut smallest cake in half; reserve second half for another use. For brim, cut 6-inch-diameter half-circle from cardboard. Tint ½ cup frosting with black food coloring. Frost brim; attach to half cake. Frost cake; place on head. Decorate as desired.

Yield: Makes 12 servings.

BUTTERCREAM FROSTING

- ½ cup (1 stick) butter or margarine, at room temperature
- 1 box (1 pound) sifted confectioners' sugar
- 3 to 4 tablespoons water
  Pinch salt

Cream butter in medium bowl; gradually beat in confectioners' sugar, water, and salt until frosting is creamy smooth. Use as directed.

Yield: Makes 2¼ cups frosting.

ROYAL ICING

- 3 tablespoons meringue powder
- 4 cups confectioners' sugar
- 6 tablespoons warm water

1. In medium bowl, combine meringue powder, confectioners' sugar, and water.

2. Beat with an electric mixer 7 to 10 minutes or until icing is stiff.

Yield: Makes 3 cups.

GINGERBREAD COOKIE MITTS

- 3 cups all-purpose flour
- 1 teaspoon baking soda
- ½ teaspoon salt
- 2 teaspoons ground ginger
- 1 teaspoon ground cinnamon
- ½ teaspoon grated nutmeg
- ¼ teaspoon ground cloves
- ¾ cup firmly packed dark-brown sugar
- ¾ cup (1½ sticks) unsalted butter, cut into pieces
- ¼ cup unsulfured molasses
- ¼ cup honey
- 1 egg
  Royal Icing (recipe, this page)
  Assorted food-coloring pastes

1. In medium bowl, sift together flour, baking soda, salt, ginger, cinnamon, nutmeg, and cloves until blended.

2. In food processor, combine brown sugar and butter. Whirl until mixture is smooth and creamy, about 1 minute. Add molasses, honey, and egg. Whirl until blended. Add flour mixture. Pulse with on-off motion just until dough clumps together.

3. Scrape dough onto sheet of plastic wrap; press together to form flat disk. Wrap; chill for 2 hours or overnight.

*P*iped with red and white icing, Gingerbread Cookie Mitts are a delectable treat for the tree. (Opposite) Kids will sing the praises of chocolaty Tra-La-Lollipops they make by themselves.

4. Heat oven to 350°. Lightly grease baking sheets.

5. Roll out dough onto floured surface to 1/4-inch thickness. Cut out cookies using mitten-shaped cookie cutter. Place 1/2 inch apart on prepared baking sheets. Make a hole in base of each mitten with a drinking straw.

6. Bake in 350° oven for 12 to 14 minutes or until cookie edges begin to darken. Cool on baking sheets for a few minutes; transfer cookies to wire racks to cool completely.

7. Make Royal Icing. Divide icing between 2 bowls; tint one bowl red. For colored mittens, use an offset spatula to coat cookies with icing. Let dry. Fill pastry bags with remaining icing. Pipe designs onto cookies. Let dry.

8. For cookie ornaments, cut a 10-inch length of jute twine for each cookie. String through cookie holes; knot ends together to make hanging loop.

Yield: Makes about twenty-one 3-inch cookies.

TRA-LA-LOLLIPOPS

  1 cup semisweet chocolate chips
  1 cup white chocolate chips
     Assorted sprinkles and candies

1. Line 2 baking sheets with waxed paper or foil. Working with one type of chocolate at a time, place chips in a resealable plastic bag. Microwave at 50-percent power, squeezing bag of chocolate occasionally, until completely melted, about 2 minutes.

2. Place 4 lollipop sticks on lined baking sheet about 2 inches apart. Snip a small corner from bag and pipe desired shape over stick, leaving a few inches of the stick free on the bottom. Decorate with sprinkles and candies. Continue with remaining chocolate and candies. Let harden in fridge for about 15 minutes.

3. Peel lollipop from waxed paper. Place in goody bag and tie with ribbon for a great Christmas treat.

Yield: Makes about 8 pops.

1.

2.

3.

COOKIE BOX

- 3 cups all-purpose flour
- 1 teaspoon baking soda
- 1/2 teaspoon salt
- 1 cup vegetable shortening
- 1/2 cup lightly packed brown sugar
- 1/2 cup granulated sugar
- 2 large eggs
- 1 teaspoon vanilla
- 2 cups chocolate chips
  - Red and green regular and mini candy-coated chocolates
  - Nonpareils
  - Red, green, and white sprinkles

1. Heat oven to 350°.

2. Sift the flour, baking soda, and salt in a bowl. Cream the shortening and sugars in a large bowl. Add the eggs and vanilla and beat well. Add the flour mixture and beat until well combined.

3. Divide dough into sixths. Roll each piece into a 1/4-inch-thick square on a lightly floured sheet of foil. Trim to a 5 1/2-inch square. Transfer foil and dough to a baking sheet.

4. Bake in 350° oven about 12 to 15 minutes or until golden brown and firm.

5. Place 1 cup of the chocolate chips in a resealable bag. Microwave chips on 50-percent power for 1 minute. Increase power to high and microwave for 30 seconds longer. If chocolate is not completely melted, microwave for 10 seconds longer. Snip a small piece from one corner. Pipe chocolate in a decorative design over cookie and use it as the "glue" for the candies. Decorate 5 squares as desired. Let dry in a cool place until chocolate is set, about 30 minutes.

6. Use the plain cookie as the base of the box. Microwave the remaining chocolate chips in a resealable bag. Snip a larger piece from one corner. Pipe chocolate along edges of base cookie. Pipe chocolate along vertical edges of side cookies. Stand side cookies on base and support sides with cans or cups. Let cookie box dry at least 1 hour. Pipe additional chocolate along seams to secure, adding more candies if desired. Fill with assorted candies and cover with decorated top cookie.

Let the kids decorate edible Cookie Boxes with colorful candies; fill with goodies and give out as party favors.

A CUTE QUARTET OF CUPCAKES

Jolly Santa:

 Pink icing
 1 cupcake
 1 black licorice dot
 2 large candy-coated mints
 1 red jelly bean
 11 mini marshmallows
 1 inch red and 1½ inches black
  shoestring licorice
 Red fruit leather

Frost cupcake. Cut licorice dot in half. Use a small dot of icing to attach licorice dot pieces to mints for the eyes. Use red jelly bean for the nose. Cut one marshmallow in half lengthwise for the mustache. Use red licorice for the mouth. Cut stocking cap shape from fruit leather; place on top edge of cupcake. Cut the other marshmallows crosswise. Use 14 halves for the beard and 6 halves for stocking cap. Cut small pieces of black licorice for eyelashes.

Sweet Elf:

 Pink icing
 1 cupcake
 3 pieces pink taffy or fruit chews
 2 blue candy-coated chocolates
 2 peppermint swirl candies
 1½ inches *each* red and black
  shoestring licorice
 3 spearmint leaf candies

Frost cupcake. Shape 2 pieces taffy into ears. Shape third piece into a disk for the nose. Use 2 blue chocolates for eyes. Use 2 peppermints for the cheeks. Use red licorice for the mouth. Cut small pieces of black licorice for eyelashes. Cut spearmint leaves in half lengthwise and attach on the top part of the cupcake for a hat.

Friendly Frosty:

 White icing
 1 cupcake
 1 large chocolate-coated
  peppermint patty
 1 spearmint leaf candy
 3 red mini candy-coated chocolates
 1 black jelly bean
 1 orange gumdrop
 5 brown mini candy-coated
  chocolates
 Red fruit leather

Frost cupcake. Cut a third of the width from a peppermint patty. Use a small dot of icing to attach the small piece on top of the other. Press slightly on the angle for the hat. Decorate with small pieces of spearmint and red chocolates for holly on hat. Cut black jelly bean in half and use for the eyes. Cut a triangular piece of orange gumdrop and use for the nose. Use brown chocolates for the mouth. Cut 2 strips of fruit leather for scarf; press along bottom edge of cupcake.

Smiley Rudolph:

 Milk-chocolate icing
 1 cupcake
 2 pretzels
 2 chocolate caramels
 2 large candy-coated mints
 2 green mini candy-coated
  chocolates
 1 red jelly bean
 1 piece pink taffy or fruit chew

Frost cupcake. Trim 2 pretzels and use for antlers. Shape chocolate caramels into 2 small ears. Use a small dot of icing to attach 2 green chocolates to mints for the eyes. Use red jelly bean for the nose. Roll bits of taffy into 2 strips for the mouth.

Delight kids with our cheery quartet of cupcakes: a jolly Santa, a sweet-as-can-be elf, a friendly snowman, and a smiley reindeer. Make them with your favorite cake mix, then frost and decorate cleverly with candies. You'll have as much fun making these cupcakes as the kids will eating them!

Baking lots of cookies is a snap if you try our time-saving technique: Mix up the dough for Vanilla Sugar Cookies (lower right); roll out, cut into shapes, and decorate before baking. Then create five scrumptious variations (clockwise from lower left), all using the same basic recipe! Pecan Crescents are a Christmas classic, or add lemon zest and chopped fruit for Lemon-Fig Biscotti. Chocoholics will love Heavenly Chocolate Cookies. Fresh ginger gives Ginger Spice Drops a tangy zing, and Sesame Jewels have rich flavor.

cookies! cookies!

MORE COOKIES, PLEASE! DROPPED, ROLLED, PIPED, OR SLICED — COOKIES OF ALL SHAPES AND SIZES ARE SIMPLY IRRESISTIBLE. STOCK YOUR HOLIDAY PANTRY WITH LOTS OF EXTRAS FOR MUNCHING, GIFTS, OR DROP-IN COMPANY.

VANILLA SUGAR COOKIES

- 1½ cups all-purpose flour
- ½ teaspoon baking powder
- ¼ teaspoon salt
- ½ cup (1 stick) unsalted butter
- ¾ cup granulated sugar
- 1 egg
- ½ teaspoon vanilla
  Colored sprinkles, sugars, jimmies and gumdrops (optional)

1. Stir together flour, baking powder, and salt in medium-size bowl.
2. Beat butter, sugar, egg, and vanilla in bowl until well blended. Stir in flour mixture. Gather dough together and shape into ball; wrap and refrigerate several hours or overnight.
3. Heat oven to 350°. Lightly spray baking sheets with nonstick vegetable-oil cooking spray.
4. Roll out dough with lightly floured rolling pin on lightly floured surface to ⅜-inch thickness. Cut into cookies with 2½-inch holiday-shaped cookie cutters. Place cookies on prepared baking sheets, spacing 1½ inches apart. Decorate with colored sprinkles, sugars, jimmies, and gumdrops, if you wish.
5. Bake in 350° oven 10 to 12 minutes or until lightly browned around edges. Remove cookies to wire racks to cool.
Yield: Makes about 3 dozen cookies.

VANILLA SUGAR COOKIE DOUGH VARIATIONS

Ginger Spice Drops: Add 2 tablespoons *each* grated fresh ginger and molasses, ¾ teaspoon ground cinnamon, and ¼ teaspoon ground allspice to butter mixture in Step 2. Drop by rounded teaspoonfuls, 2 inches apart, onto prepared baking sheets. Bake 10 to 12 minutes or until lightly browned around edges. Prepare Vanilla Glaze. Tint one-quarter of glaze with red food coloring and one-quarter with green. Spread cookies with white glaze. Drizzle with colored glaze.

Vanilla Glaze: Gradually stir 1 to 2 tablespoons milk into 1 cup confectioners' sugar in small bowl until smooth and good glazing consistency. Stir in ¼ teaspoon vanilla or lemon juice.
Yield: Makes 3½ dozen cookies.

Sesame Jewels: Add ¼ cup *each* flour and toasted sesame seeds to flour mixture in Step 1. Roll 2 teaspoonfuls dough into ball for each cookie; roll in toasted sesame seeds. Flatten slightly; place glacé cherry half in center of each. Bake 12 to 14 minutes or until lightly firm to touch.
Yield: Makes about 4 dozen cookies.

Pecan Crescents: Add 1 cup finely ground toasted pecans to flour mixture in Step 1. Substitute confectioners' sugar for granulated sugar and 2 egg yolks for whole egg in Step 2. Dough will be crumbly, so knead together briefly. Pinch 2 level teaspoonfuls of dough into a crescent for each cookie. Bake 12 minutes or until lightly browned. Transfer to wire racks to cool. Dust with confectioners' sugar.
Yield: Makes about 4 dozen cookies.

Heavenly Chocolate Cookies: Reduce flour to 1 cup and add ¼ cup unsweetened cocoa powder to flour mixture in Step 1. In Step 2, stir ½ cup *each* pecans, walnuts, semisweet chocolate chunks, and white chocolate chips into butter mixture along with the flour mixture. Drop by rounded tablespoonfuls, 2 inches apart, onto prepared baking sheets. Bake 12 to 14 minutes or until set and lightly firm to touch.
Yield: Makes about 2¼ dozen cookies.

Lemon-Fig Biscotti: Substitute ¼ teaspoon lemon extract for vanilla. Add 1 tablespoon grated lemon zest to butter mixture in Step 2. Stir in 1 cup chopped dried figs and ½ cup chopped walnuts along with flour mixture in Step 2. Divide dough in half. Shape each half into a 12 x 1-inch log. Bake for 25 minutes or until lightly firm to touch. Cool on racks. Slice diagonally into ⅝-inch-thick slices. Bake slices 15 minutes. Cool on racks. Melt creamy-white melting wafers following package directions. Dip the end of each biscotti in the melted wafers, then in sprinkles.
Yield: Makes about 3½ dozen cookies.

Cut out playful shapes for Tree and Animal Cookies ... both decorative and delicious! (Right) *Glaze whimsical cookie critters and sponge with tinted frosting; dangle from bows.* (Below) *Outline Yule-tree shapes with green frosting and stack in threes. Wait to see who can eat just one!*

TREE AND ANIMAL COOKIES

- 2 cups all-purpose flour
- 1/4 teaspoon baking soda
- 1/4 teaspoon salt
- 1/2 cup (1 stick) butter or margarine, softened
- 1/2 cup sugar
- 1 tablespoon grated orange zest
- 1 egg
- 1 tablespoon orange juice
  Royal Icing (recipe follows)
  Paste food coloring

1. In a small bowl, combine flour, baking soda, and salt. Beat butter, sugar, zest, egg, and juice in large bowl until light and fluffy. Stir in flour mixture. Shape dough into two 8-inch disks. Wrap in plastic wrap. Refrigerate at least 2 hours.

2. Heat oven to 375°. Roll out dough on lightly floured surface to 1/8-inch thickness. Cut into desired shapes. Place 1 inch apart on lightly greased baking sheets. Reroll scraps as needed. To hang cookies as decorations, punch out holes with drinking straw.

3. Bake in 375° oven 8 to 10 minutes or until very lightly browned on top. Remove to wire racks to cool.

4. Decorate tree cookies as pictured with green Royal Icing. For animal cookies, thin 1 cup Royal Icing with water to consistency of sour cream. Frost cookies; let dry. For color, tint 3 tablespoons thinned icing with food coloring to desired shade. Sponge on colors with small pieces of natural sponge or crumpled paper toweling. Let dry.

Royal Icing: Using packaged meringue powder, prepare 1 recipe Royal Icing according to package directions. Makes 3 to 4 cups. Meringue powder is available in stores where baking supplies are sold.

Yield: Makes about 2 1/2 dozen 3-inch rounds OR twenty-six 4 1/2-inch trees OR 2 1/2 dozen 4 1/2-inch animals.

Who could resist this frosty fellow! A melt-in-your-mouth Meringue Snowman, dressed in a top hat made from licorice candies and a fruit-leather scarf, is as fun to look at as it is to eat.

MERINGUE SNOWMEN

- 2 egg whites
- 1/8 teaspoon cream of tartar
- 2/3 cup sugar
- 10 licorice gumdrops
- 16 licorice coins
- 1/2 cup Royal Icing (recipe, this page)
  Red fruit leather
- 3 orange jelly-candy slices

1. Heat oven to 250°. Lightly spray 1 baking sheet with nonstick vegetable-oil cooking spray.

2. In small bowl, with electric mixer at high speed, beat egg whites and cream of tartar until soft peaks form.

3. Sprinkle in sugar, 1 tablespoon at a time, beating until sugar dissolves and firm peaks form.

4. Spoon meringue into large pastry bag fitted with 1/2-inch plain round tip. Pipe ten 2-inch balls of meringue, holding tip 1/2 inch off baking sheet, piping without moving tip. Pipe a 1 1/4-inch ball on top of each 2-inch ball, using same technique. Repeat, piping a 3/4-inch ball on top of each double ball.

5. Bake snowmen in 250° oven for 25 minutes. Turn off oven; leave oven door slightly ajar (prop open with wooden spoon). Let Meringue Snowmen stand at least 6 hours or overnight.

6. To make hats, attach 10 licorice gumdrops to licorice coins using Royal Icing; let harden. Attach hats to snowmen's heads with Royal Icing, trimming heads slightly with serrated knife, if needed.

7. Cut 8 x 3/8-inch strip red fruit leather for each scarf; notch ends. Attach with Royal Icing.

8. For eyes and buttons, roll out licorice coins and cut out 40 small dots with 1/4-inch plain pastry tip. Attach with Royal Icing. For "carrot" noses, cut out 10 small slivers of orange jelly candies. Attach with Royal Icing.

Yield: Makes 10 snowmen.

MAPLE-NUT NESTS

  1 cup (2 sticks) unsalted butter
$1/2$ cup sugar
  1 egg
  1 teaspoon vanilla
$2^{1/2}$ cups all-purpose flour
$1^{1/3}$ cups finely chopped walnuts
$1/4$ cup maple syrup
     Red and green glacé cherries, cut
       into slivers

1. Heat oven to 350°. In large bowl, with electric mixer at high speed, beat butter and sugar until fluffy. Beat in egg and vanilla. Stir in flour, one-third at a time, blending to make soft dough.
2. Measure out $1/3$ cup dough. In small bowl, mix with walnuts and maple syrup until well blended; reserve.
3. Fit pastry bag with small star tip; fill bag with remaining dough. Press out into $1^{1/2}$-inch rings on large ungreased baking sheets. Fill center of each cookie with 1 teaspoon nut mixture; decorate with glacé cherries.
4. Bake in 350° oven for 12 minutes or until lightly golden at edges. Remove cookies carefully from baking sheets to wire racks; cool completely. Store between sheets of waxed paper in airtight container for up to 2 weeks; freeze up to 1 month.
Yield: Makes about 6 dozen nests.

COCONUT-ALMOND
MACAROONS

  3 cups sliced almonds
  4 cups sweetened flaked coconut
$1^{1/2}$ cups sugar
  6 egg whites, divided
$1/4$ teaspoon almond extract
  2 cups semisweet chocolate chips
  2 tablespoons solid vegetable
     shortening OR vegetable oil

1. Heat oven to 325°. Place almonds in single layer on baking sheet. Bake for 8 to 10 minutes or until golden. Remove almonds; cool and crumble coarsely. Line 2 baking sheets with foil and lightly spray with nonstick vegetable-oil cooking spray.
2. In saucepan, combine coconut, sugar,

and 4 egg whites. Cook over low heat, stirring constantly, for about 6 minutes or until mixture thickens slightly; do not simmer. Remove from heat; stir in almond extract, almonds, and remaining 2 egg whites.
3. Drop rounded measuring teaspoonfuls of mixture onto prepared baking sheets.
4. Bake in 325° oven for 25 to 30 minutes or until macaroons are golden. Cool completely on foil, then peel off macaroons.
5. In small, heavy saucepan, melt chocolate and shortening over low heat, stirring until smooth. Dip macaroons into melted chocolate; place on baking sheet lined with waxed paper. Let stand at least 1 hour or until chocolate is set. Store between sheets of waxed paper in airtight container for up to 2 weeks; freeze up to 1 month.
Yield: Makes about 5 dozen macaroons.

HAZELNUT SHORTBREADS

  3 cups cake flour OR all-purpose
     flour
$3/4$ cup confectioners' sugar
$1/2$ cup hazelnuts, toasted and ground
$1/4$ teaspoon salt
$1^{1/4}$ cups ($2^{1/2}$ sticks) unsalted butter,
     cut into small pieces
  2 squares (1 ounce each)
     semisweet chocolate, melted
     (optional)

1. Heat oven to 325°. In medium-size bowl, stir together flour, confectioners' sugar, hazelnuts, and salt.
2. Cut butter into flour mixture with pastry blender until mixture resembles coarse meal. Knead until mixture holds together. Divide in half.
3. Place each half on ungreased baking sheet. Pat out each into 9-inch circle; crimp edges. Cut each circle into 12 equal wedges, but do not separate. Bake in 325° oven for 30 to 35 minutes or until golden brown. Drizzle chocolate, if desired, over hot shortbreads. Cool 10 minutes. Recut to separate wedges. Cool completely.
Yield: Makes 2 dozen shortbread wedges.

SESAME JAM BARS

$1/3$ cup sesame seeds
$3/4$ cup ($1^{1/2}$ sticks) unsalted butter
$3/4$ cup firmly packed light-brown
     sugar
$1/4$ cup honey
  1 egg yolk
  1 teaspoon vanilla
  2 cups all-purpose flour
$1/2$ teaspoon baking powder
$1/2$ teaspoon salt
$1/2$ cup cherry jam OR apricot jam

1. Heat oven to 375°. Place sesame seeds in 13 x 9 x 2-inch baking pan. Bake in 375° oven for 6 to 8 minutes or until golden and fragrant. Place on plate to cool. Line same pan with foil; spray with nonstick vegetable-oil cooking spray.
2. In food processor, whirl butter, brown sugar, honey, egg yolk, and vanilla until smooth. Add flour, baking powder, and salt. Whirl just until combined.
3. Scrape dough into prepared baking pan, spreading level. Sprinkle evenly with seeds. Score into rectangles (cutting lengthwise into thirds and crosswise into $1^{1/2}$-inch widths) or into diamonds.
4. Bake in 375° oven for 20 minutes. Using teaspoon measure, make indentation in center of each bar. Spoon $1/2$ teaspoon jam into each.
5. Bake in 375° oven for 5 minutes more. Cool completely on rack. Remove from pan. Cut into bars. Store in airtight container in cool spot for up to 2 weeks.
Yield: Makes about 24 bars.

Dress up your cookies for the holidays — cut out a special shape, add a fruity filling, dip into or drizzle with chocolate. (Opposite, clockwise from top right) Assemble a sampler of favorites: rich Fig Thumbprints, crunchy Sesame Jam Bars, spicy Cinnamon-Chocolate Dominoes, airy Maple-Nut Nests, chewy Coconut-Almond Macaroons, and buttery Hazelnut Shortbreads.

FIG THUMBPRINTS

Fig Filling:

- 4 ounces Calimyrna figs
- 2 tablespoons granulated sugar
- 2 teaspoons grated orange zest
- 1/4 cup water
- 1 tablespoon orange juice
- 1 tablespoon brandy (optional)

Cookies:

- 1/2 cup (1 stick) unsalted butter
- 1/3 cup firmly packed light-brown sugar
- 1 egg
- 1/2 teaspoon vanilla
- 1 1/4 cups all-purpose flour
- 1/2 teaspoon salt
- 1/2 to 3/4 cup ground walnuts

1. Prepare Filling: In food processor, whirl figs, sugar, and orange zest until puréed.
2. In small saucepan, mix fig mixture, water, juice, and, if desired, brandy. Bring to boiling. Lower heat; simmer, uncovered, until thickened, about 5 minutes. Cool to room temperature.
3. Prepare Cookies: In large bowl, beat butter until creamy. Gradually beat in brown sugar until light and fluffy. Beat in egg and vanilla. Stir in flour and salt just until dough holds together. Refrigerate dough until firm, about 30 minutes.
4. Heat oven to 350°. Shape dough into 1-inch balls. Roll balls in walnuts to coat. Place 1 inch apart on ungreased baking sheets. With thumb, make indentation in center of each ball.
5. Bake in 350° oven for 12 to 15 minutes or until lightly browned. Remove to wire racks to cool.
6. Just before serving, fill each cookie with Fig Filling or use a favorite jam.
Yield: Makes about 2 1/2 dozen cookies.

CINNAMON-CHOCOLATE DOMINOES

- 2 cups all-purpose flour
- 2 teaspoons ground cinnamon
- 1/2 cup (1 stick) unsalted butter or margarine
- 2/3 cup sugar
- 1/2 teaspoon vanilla
- 2 egg yolks
- 2 tablespoons dark corn syrup
- 3 squares (1 ounce each) semisweet chocolate, melted
- 1/2 cup Royal Icing (recipe, page 101)

1. In small bowl, combine flour and cinnamon.
2. In large bowl, beat butter, sugar, vanilla, egg yolks, and corn syrup until fluffy. Mix in chocolate. Stir in flour mixture until well blended.
3. Divide mixture in half. Shape each half into 8-inch disk. Wrap in plastic wrap or waxed paper. Refrigerate for at least 2 hours or until firm enough to handle easily.
4. Heat oven to 350°. Grease baking sheets.
5. Roll out 1 disk at a time on lightly floured surface to 3/8-inch thickness. Cut dough into 2 1/2 x 1 1/4-inch rectangles. Place 1 inch apart on prepared baking sheets. Make indentation, with back of knife blade, into each cookie to divide in half crosswise; don't cut all the way through.
6. Bake in 350° oven for 10 minutes or until slightly firm. Remove from baking sheets to wire racks to cool. Using pastry bag fitted with small writing tip, add domino dots with Royal Icing.
Yield: Makes about 6 dozen cookies.

STAINED-GLASS COOKIES

- 1 cup (2 sticks) unsalted butter
- 2/3 cup sugar
- 1 egg yolk
- 1 teaspoon vanilla
- 1/2 teaspoon lemon extract
- 2 3/4 cups unsifted all-purpose flour
- 1/2 teaspoon salt
- 1/2 teaspoon baking powder
  About 11 rolls colored doughnut-shaped hard candies (such as Lifesavers)

1. Heat oven to 350°. Line baking sheets with foil. Spray with nonstick vegetable-oil cooking spray.
2. In large bowl, beat butter and sugar until fluffy. Add egg yolk, vanilla, and lemon extract. Beat until blended.
3. In small bowl, whisk together flour, salt, and baking powder. Stir into butter mixture with wooden spoon until dough comes together. Wrap in plastic wrap. Refrigerate for at least 15 minutes.
4. Separate hard candies into individual colors. Break into 1/4-inch pieces with hammer or rolling pin. Reserve each color separately.
5. Using about one-fourth of dough at a time, roll out dough between 2 sheets of waxed paper to 1/8-inch thickness. Cut out cookies with 3-inch cookie cutter. Transfer to prepared baking sheets with pancake turner. If planning to hang cookies, make hole in each cookie near edge with drinking straw or large, plain pastry tip. Cut out shapes for stained glass in each cookie with small cutters in different shapes or use small knife. Fill holes with broken candy.
6. Bake in 350° oven for 10 minutes or until cookies are lightly browned and candy has melted. Allow to cool on foil, then carefully peel off. Store in airtight container for up to 10 days.
Yield: Makes 3 to 4 dozen cookies.

Cut Stained-Glass Cookies in a variety of silhouettes with festive windows; bake with crushed hard candies in the openings to create the "glass." Set out for snacking or tie on ribbon hangers and display them in a window to catch the light.

tasteful gifts

FRESH FROM YOUR KITCHEN, THESE TASTEFUL
OFFERINGS WILL PLEASE EVERYONE ON YOUR LIST.
FROM CRUNCHY MUNCHIES TO DANDY CANDIES,
THERE'S NO NICER WAY TO SHOW YOUR LOVE THAN
WITH A DELICIOUS TREAT YOU'VE MADE YOURSELF!

HERBY TOMATO-PINE NUT QUICK BREAD

- 3 cups all-purpose flour
- 1/2 cup grated Parmesan cheese
- 1/2 cup pine nuts
- 2 teaspoons baking powder
- 1 teaspoon baking soda
- 1 teaspoon *each* crumbled dried basil, thyme, rosemary
- 1/2 teaspoon salt
- 1/2 teaspoon freshly ground black pepper
- 1 1/2 cups buttermilk
- 3 tablespoons tomato paste
- 1/4 cup vegetable oil
- 1 egg

1. Heat oven to 350°. Grease 9 x 5-inch loaf pan. Sprinkle with flour; tap out any excess.
2. Combine the 3 cups flour, Parmesan cheese, pine nuts, baking powder, baking soda, basil, thyme, rosemary, salt, and pepper in large bowl.
3. Whisk together buttermilk, tomato paste, oil, and egg in medium-size bowl. Add to flour mixture; stir until no traces of flour remain. Spoon batter into prepared pan.
4. Bake in 350° oven for 50 minutes or until wooden pick inserted in center comes out clean. Transfer pan to wire rack to cool for 10 minutes. Turn bread out onto rack to cool completely.
Yield: Makes 12 slices.

MULLED SPICE PACKETS

- 4 oranges
- 1 piece fresh ginger (5 inches)
- 10 cinnamon sticks
- 60 allspice berries
- 30 whole cloves

1. Heat oven to 150°.
2. Slice the oranges and ginger a scant 1/4 inch thick (you should have 40 orange slices and 20 ginger slices). Arrange in a single layer on cooling racks.
3. Place orange and ginger in oven. Prop oven door open slightly. Bake in 150° oven for 3 to 4 hours until dried. Remove from oven to cool completely.
4. Place 4 orange slices, 2 ginger slices, 1 cinnamon stick, 6 allspice berries, and 3 cloves in center of cheesecloth; tie in bundle. Use for mulled cider, wine, or grape punch.
5. For a special gift, divide ingredients among 10 decorative glass jars. Package each jar with mugs.
Yield: Makes 10 packets.
Mulled Cider: Combine 1/2 gallon cider, 1/4 cup firmly packed brown sugar, and Mulled Spice Packet in saucepan. Bring to bare simmer; simmer, covered, 10 minutes. Serve hot.

LEMON-CHILE HONEY

- 2 cups honey
- 4 strips lemon zest
- 2 tablespoons fresh lemon juice
- 3 whole dried chiles
- 1/2 teaspoon whole allspice

In saucepan, combine honey, zest, juice, chiles, and allspice. Bring to boiling. Pour into sterilized jars. Store 24 hours at room temperature before using; refrigerate for up to 3 months.
Note: Honey may crystallize when refrigerated, but can be microwaved to bring back to liquid.
Yield: Makes 2 cups.

Herby Tomato-Pine Nut Quick Bread (opposite) makes a hearty hello. Put together a gift box with the makings for a fragrant mulled drink with spices, mugs, and all (above, left). Give a pretty pitcher of Lemon-Chile Honey — it's a bread spread with bite and a tantalizing taste for tea!

TEX-MEX POPCORN

8	cups popped popcorn
1	cup pretzel sticks
1	cup bite-size toasted corn cereal
1/4	cup butter or margarine, melted
1	teaspoon chili powder
1/2	teaspoon garlic powder
1/4	teaspoon ground cumin
1/4	teaspoon onion salt
1/8	teaspoon ground hot red pepper

1. Heat oven to 275°. Combine popcorn, pretzels, and cereal in large roasting pan. Combine butter, chili powder, garlic powder, cumin, onion salt, and ground red pepper in small bowl. Pour over popcorn mixture; toss to coat.
2. Bake in 275° oven 30 minutes, stirring occasionally. Let cool to room temperature.
3. Store popcorn mix in airtight container at room temperature up to 3 days.
Yield: Makes about 8 cups.

MAPLE-GLAZED SESAME POPCORN

8	cups hot-air popped popcorn
3/4	cup maple syrup
3	tablespoons light-brown sugar
1/8	teaspoon ground cinnamon
1 1/2	tablespoons unsalted butter
1 1/2	tablespoons sesame seeds

1. Heat oven to 250°. Lightly spray very large ovenproof bowl, preferably made of glass or ceramic, and baking sheet with nonstick vegetable-oil cooking spray.
2. Add popcorn to bowl. Place in 250° oven to warm while making glaze.
3. Stir together maple syrup, brown sugar, and cinnamon in heavy small saucepan. Bring to boiling over medium heat; cook to hard-ball stage (250° on candy thermometer). Stir in butter; cook to soft-crack stage (280° on candy thermometer).
4. Remove popcorn from oven. Pour about half of glaze over popcorn, working quickly; coat popcorn by tossing with metal spoon. Sprinkle on sesame seeds; pour on remaining glaze. Toss

until coated evenly. (If mixture cools down too quickly, warm in oven until softened enough to mix.)

5. Spoon onto prepared baking sheet and spread into small clumps. Let cool before serving or packaging for gift giving.

Yield: Makes 8 cups.

PUMPKIN-SEED DIP

1	pound hulled raw pumpkin seeds
1/2	cup olive oil
1	to 2 pickled jalapeño peppers, seeded and minced
1	teaspoon ground cumin
1/4	teaspoon garlic powder
1 1/2	cups water
4	to 6 tablespoons bottled lime juice OR lemon juice
2	tablespoons white vinegar
1 1/2	teaspoons salt
1/2	teaspoon ground black pepper

1. Heat oven to 350°. Spread seeds in shallow pan in single layer. Bake in 350° oven 12 minutes or until golden and crunchy; cool.

2. Combine seeds, oil, jalapeño pepper, cumin, garlic powder, water, lime juice, vinegar, salt, and black pepper in food processor or blender. Whirl until a thick purée, scraping down sides of bowl as necessary.

3. Add additional water if needed to achieve consistency of slightly thin peanut butter. Pack into sterilized jars. Refrigerate up to 2 weeks.

Yield: Makes about 4 cups.

Toss Tex-Mex Popcorn (opposite, bottom) with pretzel sticks, toasted corn cereal, and fiery spices. For those with sweeter tooths, mix up some Maple-Glazed Sesame Popcorn (top). Cranberry Ketchup makes a delightfully different sandwich spread (above, left). Pumpkin-Seed Dip takes to breadsticks, crudités, or chips.

CRANBERRY KETCHUP

2	packages (12 ounces each) cranberries, fresh or frozen, thawed
2	medium onions, finely chopped
1	cup water
2	cinnamon sticks, broken in half
1	teaspoon mustard seeds
1	teaspoon whole allspice
1	teaspoon whole black peppercorns
2	cups sugar
1	cup cider vinegar
2 1/2	teaspoons salt

1. Bring cranberries, onions, and water to boiling in large saucepan. Lower heat; cover and simmer 20 minutes.

2. Transfer cranberry mixture to blender or food processor, working in batches if necessary. Whirl until puréed. Return mixture to saucepan. Cook over medium heat until reduced to 2 cups.

3. Tie cinnamon sticks, mustard seeds, allspice, and peppercorns in cheesecloth bag. Add to saucepan with sugar, vinegar, and salt. Cook slowly over very low heat until quite thick, stirring frequently. Remove spice bag. Pour into sterilized decorative bottles or jars. Refrigerate up to 3 weeks.

Yield: Makes about 2 cups.

CHOCOLATE-ORANGE SWIRL BREAD

- 1/3 cup sugar
- 1 package active dry yeast
- 1/4 cup warm water
- 2 1/2 to 3 cups all-purpose flour
- 1 1/2 teaspoons ground cinnamon
- 1/2 teaspoon salt
- 2 teaspoons grated orange zest
- 1/3 cup orange juice
- 1/4 cup butter or margarine, softened
- 1 egg
- 1 cup (6-ounce package) semisweet chocolate chips
  Orange Glaze (recipe follows), optional

1. Mix 1 tablespoon sugar with yeast and water in small cup. Let stand 5 minutes until bubbly.
2. Place 2 cups flour in large bowl; add remaining sugar, 1/2 teaspoon cinnamon, salt, and 1/2 teaspoon orange zest; stir to combine. Add yeast mixture, orange juice, butter, and egg. Stir with wooden spoon until well mixed.
3. Gradually stir in remaining flour to make a soft dough. Turn out on lightly floured surface; knead 10 minutes, adding more flour if necessary.
4. Place dough in large greased bowl, turning to oil top of dough. Cover with towel and let rise in warm place away from drafts until doubled in volume, about 1 hour.
5. Combine remaining 1 1/2 teaspoons orange zest and 1 teaspoon cinnamon in small bowl.
6. Punch down dough; knead briefly. Roll into a 9 x 14-inch rectangle on floured surface. Sprinkle cinnamon mixture over dough to within 1 inch of the edges. Drizzle with 1 tablespoon water. Cover with chocolate chips.
7. Grease 8-inch loaf pan. Roll up dough from short end; seal edge and fold ends under. Place, seam side down, in prepared pan. Place in warm place away from drafts until almost doubled in volume, about 45 minutes.
8. Heat oven to 350°. Bake bread 45 minutes or until crust is golden brown. Remove to wire rack; loosen around edges with metal spatula; turn out onto rack to cool.
9. When bread is cool, drizzle with Orange Glaze, if using.

Orange Glaze: Stir together 1 cup confectioners' sugar, 1/4 teaspoon grated orange zest, and 1 1/2 to 3 tablespoons orange juice in small bowl. Beat until smooth and thin enough to spread.

Note: Bread may be wrapped and frozen up to 1 month. Thaw in refrigerator and drizzle with Orange Glaze before serving. If giving as a gift, attach recipe for Orange Glaze to wrapped loaf.

Yield: Makes 1 loaf (16 servings).

PUMPKIN LOAF WITH DRIED CHERRIES

- 2 1/2 cups all-purpose flour
- 2 teaspoons baking soda
- 1 1/2 teaspoons ground cinnamon
- 1 teaspoon ground ginger
- 1/2 teaspoon salt
- 1/2 teaspoon ground cloves
- 1/4 teaspoon ground nutmeg
- 2 eggs
- 2 cups sugar
- 1/2 cup vegetable oil
- 2 cups canned pumpkin purée
- 1 cup dried cherries, raisins, or chopped pitted dates
  Confectioners' sugar, optional

1. Grease loaf pans. Heat oven to 350°.
2. Combine flour, baking soda, cinnamon, ginger, salt, cloves, and nutmeg in a small bowl; stir with fork to mix well.
3. Beat eggs, sugar, and oil with whisk in large bowl. Beat in pumpkin and cherries. Stir in dry ingredients.
4. Pour into prepared pans. Push batter into corners of pans with spatula, leaving sides slightly higher than middle.
5. Bake in 350° oven 45 minutes for large loaves or 30 minutes for smaller loaves or until wooden pick inserted in center comes out clean.
6. Cool on racks 10 minutes before removing from pans. Cool completely, then wrap in plastic or foil. (The flavor develops if you wait a day before slicing.) Loaves may also be frozen up to 2 months. If desired, sprinkle confectioners' sugar over loaves before serving.

Yield: Makes 3 loaves (6" x 3" x 2")

QUICK CHEESE BREAD

- 2 cups all-purpose flour
- 1/2 cup whole-wheat flour
- 1 tablespoon sugar
- 2 teaspoons baking powder
- 1 teaspoon salt
- 1/2 teaspoon baking soda
- 1/2 teaspoon dry mustard
- 1/4 teaspoon ground red pepper
- 4 ounces sharp Cheddar cheese, shredded (1 cup)
- 1 egg
- 1 cup buttermilk
- 1/4 cup vegetable oil

1. Heat oven to 350°.
2. Grease 8-inch loaf pan; cut waxed paper to fit bottom of pan; grease paper.
3. Mix together flours, sugar, baking powder, salt, baking soda, dry mustard, and red pepper in large bowl. Stir in all but 1/4 cup Cheddar cheese.
4. Beat egg in a 2-cup measuring cup; stir in buttermilk and oil.
5. Add liquid ingredients to dry, stirring just until moistened. Turn into prepared pan. Sprinkle with remaining cheese.
6. Bake in 350° oven 50 minutes or until wooden pick inserted in center comes out clean. Cool on rack 10 minutes before removing from pan.

Yield: Makes 1 loaf (16 servings).

Pumpkin Loaf with Dried Cherries (opposite, from top) is rich with wholesome flavor. Quick Cheese Bread is a tasty treat you can make in about an hour. Red pepper and chili powder lend a piquant punch to Spiced Nuts. Chocolate-Orange Swirl Bread is irresistible!

SPICED NUTS

- 2 cups walnut halves
- 1 cup pecan halves
- 1 cup blanched slivered almonds
- 1/2 cup butter or margarine
- 2 teaspoons chili powder
- 1 teaspoon ground cumin
  Pinch ground red pepper
- 1 teaspoon salt

1. Heat oven to 300°. Line a shallow baking pan with foil. Place walnuts, pecans, and almonds on foil.
2. Heat butter in small skillet until melted. Stir in chili powder, cumin, and red pepper. Spoon spice mixture over nuts, tossing to coat evenly.
3. Bake in 300° oven 30 to 45 minutes or until crisp and toasted. Sprinkle with salt. Let cool and store in airtight container.
Yield: Makes 3 1/2 cups.

BAG O' BEANS SOUP MIX

Bean Mixture:
- 1 cup dried kidney beans
- 1 cup dried chick-peas
- 1 cup dried navy beans
- 1 cup dried green split peas

Seasoning Packet:
- 8 tablespoons dried parsley
- 8 tablespoons vegetable bouillon granules
- 8 teaspoons dried leaf basil
- 4 teaspoons dried leaf oregano

1. Prepare Bean Mixture: Stir together kidney beans, chick-peas, navy beans, and split peas in a large bowl. Divide equally among 4 plastic bags; tie with ribbon.
2. Prepare Seasoning Packet: Combine parsley, bouillon granules, basil, and oregano in small bowl. Divide equally among 4 small plastic bags; seal.
3. To give as a gift, wrap a package of beans and a seasoning packet with soup bowls, along with dried bay leaves and the recipe for Vegetable Minestrone Soup.
Yield: Makes 4 cups mix.

VEGETABLE MINESTRONE SOUP

- 1 cup Bag O' Beans Soup Mix (recipe, this page)
- 10 cups water
- 5 cups cubed assorted vegetables, such as onions, sweet peppers, turnips, carrots, potatoes, and celery
- 1/2 cup small shaped pasta, such as elbows or mini bow ties
- 2 teaspoons salt

1. Pick over beans. Soak in water to cover overnight; drain and rinse.
2. Combine soaked beans, contents of seasoning packet, and 10 cups water in stockpot. Bring to simmering; cook, covered, 1 hour. Add vegetables, pasta, and salt. Cook, covered, 20 minutes until vegetables are tender.
Yield: Makes about 12 cups.

PEPPERED CHEESE BITES

- 3/4 cup (1 1/2 sticks) unsalted butter
- 6 ounces shredded extra-sharp Cheddar cheese (1 1/2 cups)
- 1/3 cup grated Parmesan cheese
- 1/2 teaspoon paprika
- 1/4 teaspoon salt
- 1/4 teaspoon ground white pepper
- 1 1/2 cups all-purpose flour

1. Heat oven to 350°. Combine butter, Cheddar cheese, Parmesan cheese, paprika, salt, and pepper in food processor. Whirl until blended. Add flour. Pulse with on-off motions until blended.

Present a thoughtful gift for busy families (top) — tie ribbon around pretty bowls and easy Bag O' Beans Soup Mix along with a recipe for warming Vegetable Minestrone Soup. The zesty zip of Peppered Cheese Bites (left) is the perfect treat for serious snackers. (Opposite) Everyone's favorite, Chocolate-Peanut Butter Fudge is marbled with yummy taste.

2. Put dough into cookie press, using a flower or Christmas tree shape. Press out dough onto ungreased baking sheet, spacing cookies 1 inch apart.
3. Bake in 350° oven for 14 to 16 minutes or until golden in color. Cool on wire racks; store in airtight container for up to 2 weeks or freeze up to 1 month.
Yield: Makes about 5 dozen crackers.

CHOCOLATE-PEANUT BUTTER FUDGE

   1   package (10 ounces) peanut butter chips
   $^3/_4$ cup unsalted creamy-style peanut butter
   1   jar ($7^1/_2$ ounces) marshmallow cream
   $^3/_4$ cup sugar
   $^2/_3$ cup evaporated skim milk
   2   tablespoons unsalted butter
   $^1/_4$ teaspoon salt
   8   ounces ($1^1/_4$ cups) semisweet chocolate pieces
   4   squares (1 ounce each) unsweetened chocolate
   $^1/_2$ cup peanuts, chopped (optional)

1. Line 9-inch-square pan with foil.
2. Combine peanut butter chips and peanut butter in top of double boiler set over hot, not boiling, water; stir occasionally until melted and smooth. Remove from heat; cool mixture slightly.
3. Meanwhile, combine marshmallow cream, sugar, milk, butter, and salt in medium-size heavy saucepan. Place over medium heat and bring to full rolling boil; cook, whisking occasionally, for 5 minutes. Remove from heat. Add chocolate pieces and squares, stirring constantly, until melted and smooth.
4. Pour $1^3/_4$ cups chocolate mixture into prepared pan, spreading evenly; refrigerate 5 minutes.
5. Pour slightly cooled peanut mixture over chocolate in pan. Using thin metal spatula, carefully spread over chocolate to sides of pan. Top with remaining chocolate mixture, spreading to cover the peanut butter mixture completely.

Using a thin metal spatula and gently lifting, slightly swirl the peanut-chocolate mixture in figure 8's over the entire surface. Sprinkle with chopped nuts, if you wish. Chill overnight. Cut into 64 squares.

Note: Fudge can be frozen in a tightly sealed container for up to 2 weeks.
Yield: Makes 64 squares.

ORANGE FRUITCAKE

- 2 cups all-purpose flour
- 1 teaspoon baking powder
- 1/2 teaspoon baking soda
- 1/2 teaspoon ground cinnamon
- 1/4 teaspoon salt
- 1/4 teaspoon ground nutmeg
- 3/4 cup pecans, coarsely chopped
- 3/4 cup glacé cherries, halved
- 1/2 cup golden raisins
- 1/2 cup diced candied orange peel
- 1 tablespoon grated orange zest
- 1/2 cup (1 stick) unsalted butter
- 1 1/2 cups sugar
- 2 eggs
- 3/4 cup buttermilk
- 1/2 cup strained orange juice
- 2 tablespoons orange liqueur (optional)
  Confectioners' Sugar Glaze (recipe follows)
  Orange-rind star cutouts

1. Heat oven to 350°. Coat six 4-inch individual Bundt pans (or six 4 1/2 x 2 1/2 x 1 1/2-inch mini loaf pans) and one 8 x 4 x 2-inch loaf pan with nonstick vegetable-oil cooking spray.
2. Stir together flour, baking powder, baking soda, cinnamon, salt, and nutmeg in medium-size bowl until well mixed. Combine pecans, cherries, raisins, candied orange peel, and grated zest in another bowl. Stir a few tablespoons flour mixture into pecan mixture to coat ingredients.
3. Beat together butter and 1 cup sugar in large bowl until smooth and creamy. Beat in eggs, one at a time. Beat until light and fluffy, 2 minutes. Stir in flour mixture alternately with buttermilk until blended, beginning and ending with flour. Gently stir in pecan mixture. Spoon 1/2 cup batter into each prepared Bundt or mini loaf pan; spoon remaining batter into prepared loaf pan.
4. Bake in 350° oven until wooden pick inserted in center comes out clean — 20 minutes for individual loaves, 35 minutes for large loaf.
5. Meanwhile, combine remaining 1/2 cup sugar and orange juice in small saucepan. Bring to boiling, stirring to

dissolve sugar. Remove from heat; stir in orange liqueur, if using.
6. When cakes are done, remove from oven. Let stand in pans on wire rack 10 minutes. Prick holes in cakes with long-tined fork. Spoon orange syrup over cakes. Cool until slightly warm. Remove from pans. Cool on wire rack. Drizzle top with Confectioners' Sugar Glaze and decorate with orange-rind star cutouts.
Confectioners' Sugar Glaze: Mix together 1 cup confectioners' sugar and 1 tablespoon water in a small bowl.
Yield: Makes 6 individual loaves and 1 loaf cake.

MAPLE VANILLA SWIRL FUDGE

- 2 packages (11 ounces each) premium white chocolate pieces
- 1/3 cup half-and-half
- 1/2 teaspoon maple extract
- 1 cup chopped toasted walnuts

1. Line a 10 x 7-inch baking pan with aluminum foil. Coat the foil lightly with nonstick vegetable-oil cooking spray.
2. Melt the white chocolate pieces in the top of a double boiler over hot, not boiling, water. Stir the chocolate constantly until melted. Add the half-and-half; stir until the mixture is smooth and glossy. (The mixture may look separated at first, but will become smooth and glossy as you stir the chocolate.)
3. Stir together 1 generous cup of melted white chocolate with maple extract and nuts. Alternately spoon white chocolate and maple mixtures in prepared pan; swirl together with knife. Refrigerate until set, 2 to 4 hours. Cut into 24 squares. Refrigerate for up to 1 month.
Yield: Makes 2 dozen squares.

CHOCOLATE NUT BARK

8 ounces milk chocolate,
   bittersweet chocolate, or white
   chocolate, chopped (see Note)
3/4 cup toasted pecans, almonds, or
   pistachios

1. Coat a baking sheet evenly and lightly with nonstick vegetable-oil cooking spray.

2. Melt chocolate in microwave-safe container at full power (100%) for 2 minutes. Stir until smooth. (Or heat the chocolate in the top of a double boiler over barely simmering, not boiling, water until smooth.) Stir in the chopped nuts. Scrape onto the prepared baking sheet; spreading an even layer, about an 8- to 9-inch square, distributing nuts evenly through the chocolate.

3. Let the bark stand until completely cooled. Break or cut the bark into pieces. Store the bark pieces in an airtight container in a cool, dry place up to 1 month.

4. To give as a gift, package pieces of bark in a wooden box.

Note: If using white chocolate, add 3/4 teaspoon vegetable oil in Step 2 when melting the chocolate.

Yield: Makes 12 servings.

Great for do-ahead gifts, Orange Fruitcake (opposite) offers a jump-start for the holidays. Keep an eye out for decorative containers all year long — they're perfect for presenting Chocolate Nut Bark and Maple Vanilla Swirl Fudge (right).

first impressions (pages 6-11)

BECKONING BELL (continued)

Decorating: Insert juniper and pine sprigs, pointing down, until bell is covered. Add bittersweet and berries here and there. *Moss* – Cut sheet moss to fit along edges; attach with U-pins. *"Clapper"* – Glue ornament and its cap together. Cut a short piece of ribbon, thread through loop; knot; trim ends to $1/2$". Attach ribbon to bottom of bell with T-pin. *Bow* – Tie remaining ribbon in a bow; glue to top of bell. *Hanger* – Stretch wire across back of bell; secure with U-pins. Hang on door with wreath hanger.

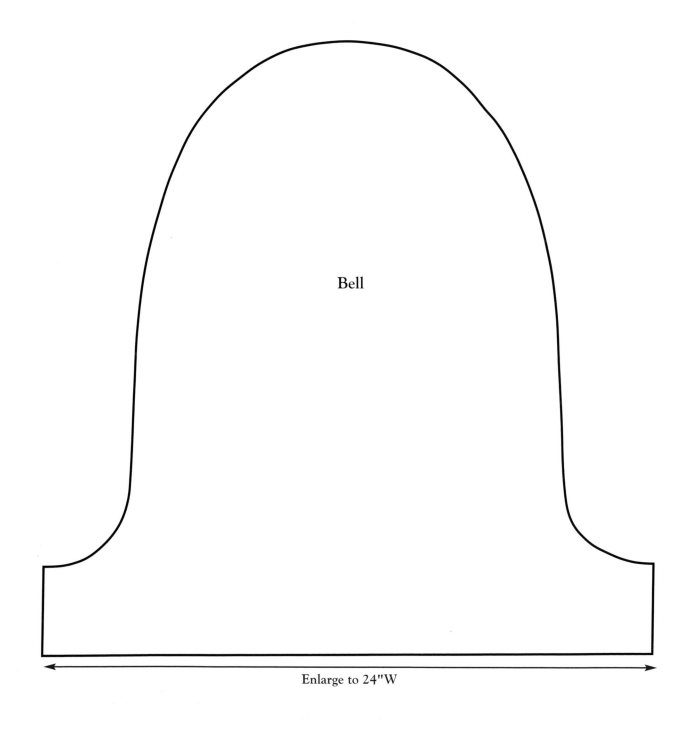

Bell

Enlarge to 24"W

GARLAND GREETING

You need: *Garland* – evergreen garland, several strands of bead garland, floral wire, ribbon bows for corners and door; *gingerbread man* – ½" plywood, jigsaw, buttons for eyes and body, brown acrylic paint, paintbrush, white dimensional fabric paint writer, ribbon bow, strip of flannel fabric for scarf, glue gun, picture hanger, finish nails, hammer.

Making garland: Holding several strands of bead garland together, wrap bead garland around evergreen garland; secure with wire.

Hanging garland and bows: Hang garland around door. Wire bows to corners. Attach bow to door.

Cutting gingerbread man: Enlarge pattern to 24"W. Use jigsaw to cut gingerbread man from plywood.

Painting: Paint man brown. Add "icing" with paint writer.

Finishing: Glue buttons to man. Wrap flannel strip around neck. Glue ribbon bow to flannel. Nail picture hanger to top back of man. Attach man to door.

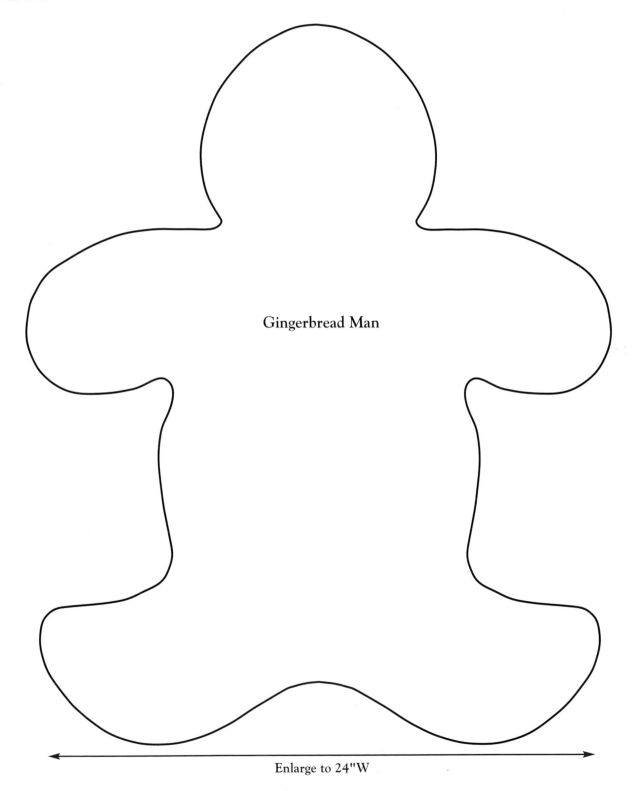

Gingerbread Man

Enlarge to 24"W

SANTA BANNER

Size: 20$\frac{1}{2}$" x 33$\frac{1}{2}$"

You need: Fabric – 1 yd blue, $\frac{1}{2}$ yd red, $\frac{1}{2}$ yd white, $\frac{1}{4}$ yd yellow, $\frac{1}{4}$ yd ivory, pink scraps; paper-backed fusible web; aluminum foil; dimensional fabric paint writers – black, white, yellow, red, pink; 1" dowel.

Preparing banner: From blue fabric, cut 21$\frac{1}{2}$" x 34$\frac{1}{2}$" banner; stitch $\frac{1}{2}$" hem on all edges.

Preparing appliqués: Enlarge patterns (this page and page 119). Fuse web to wrong sides of remaining colors of fabric. *From red* – Cut hat. *From white* – Cut beard (cut edge in fringe as shown on pattern), mustache, hat trim, and pom-pom. *From yellow* – Cut 10 stars. *From ivory* – Cut face and nose. From pink, cut cheeks.

Assembling: Working on a large, flat surface, arrange appliqués on front of banner with stars at least 4" from top edge. Place pieces of aluminum foil under edges of appliqués that extend past edges of banner and under fringed edge of beard. Fuse appliqués in place; peel off aluminum foil while appliqués are still warm. Trim star appliqués even with edge of banner.

Painting: Outline appliqué edges and add details with paint; add black eyes with white highlights. Let dry.

Finishing: Turn under 3$\frac{1}{2}$" on upper edge of banner; stitch near edge to form casing. Slide dowel through casing to support banner.

DRAMATIC DOME (continued)

Decorating: Glue moss all over dome, filling in any uneven areas to create a smooth surface. *Greens* – Insert sprigs of pine and boxwood securely through moss into foam until dome is almost covered (leave areas of moss peeking through). *Ornaments* – Secure to dome with U-pins, including tassel at bottom. *Hanger* – Stretch wire across back of dome; secure with U-pins. *Ribbon* – Tape a length on door, from inside top edge to front of door, end concealed behind dome. (**Note:** Ribbon is decorative; do not use to support dome.) Tie remaining ribbon in a bow; glue to top of dome. Hang dome on wreath hanger or nail tapped in door.

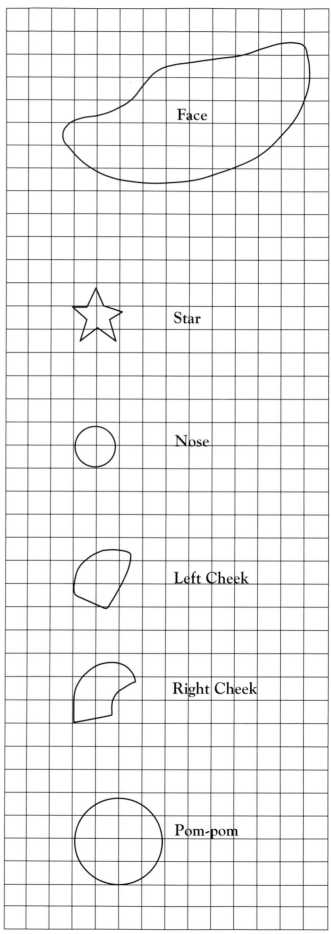

Santa Banner   1 square = 1"

Face

Star

Nose

Left Cheek

Right Cheek

Pom-pom

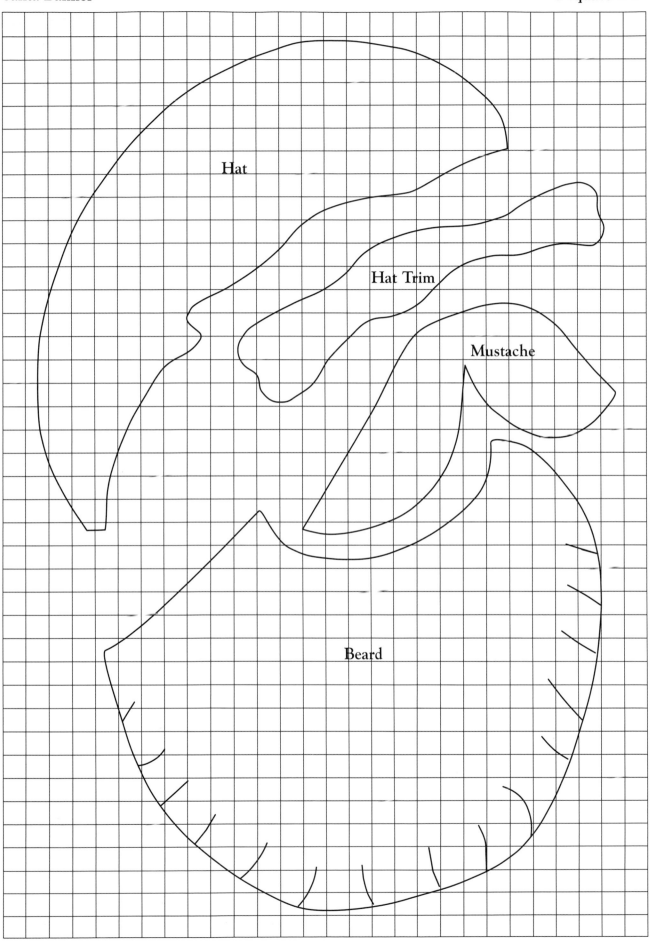

Hat

Hat Trim

Mustache

Beard

welcome one and all
(pages 12-19)

LIME TOPIARY

You need: Heavy urn; plastic foam topiary form with trunk and base; serrated knife; glue gun; sheet moss; wood floral picks; about 50 limes; about 12 pinecones; cedar greenery; gold spray paint; preserved lemon leaves.

Preparing: Paint leaves and pinecones gold; let dry. Use knife to trim bottom of topiary form base to fit firmly into urn. Glue base into urn. Glue moss to cover base, using small pieces to cover any empty spaces.

Decorating: Push floral pick through each lime so point protrudes at base. Glue an additional floral pick to each pinecone. Starting at bottom of cone and working toward top, insert rows of limes into cone until cone is covered, inserting pinecones randomly among limes, forming topiary.

Finishing: Insert greenery and some leaves among limes. Arrange remaining leaves around base of topiary.

FRUITED WREATH

You need: Fresh magnolia leaves; dried wheat stalks; 22-gauge green wire; glue gun; 18" grapevine wreath; wood floral picks; pomegranates; craft knife; freeze-dried lemons, limes, crab apples, and artichokes; dried orange slices and orange pomanders; dried berry clusters.

Preparing wreath: Hold several leaves together by their stems, forming a cluster. Wrap stems with wire. Make clusters from wheat in same way. Glue clusters to wreath in overlapping layers.

Embellishing: Make vertical cuts in lemon and lime rinds. Insert floral picks into center of whole fruits and into edges of orange slices. Place floral picks along stems of berry clusters; wrap with wire. Apply glue to floral picks; insert into wreath.

Finishing: Cut 12" of wire; fold in half lengthwise. Twist together to form hanging loop. Twist end of loop around top of wreath.

STAINED-GLASS QUILT

Size: 33" x 33"

You need: Fabrics – $^1/_2$ yd white-on-white print for background; $^1/_3$ yd gold/black print for sashing; scraps of solid red for corner squares and holly berries, green print for poinsettia leaves, and yellow print for poinsettia center; 1 yd muslin; Christmas-print fabrics – 1 yd for backing; fat quarter each of red print for poinsettia petals, green print for holly leaves, print for sashing on center square; $^1/_4$ yd each of 4 prints for crazy-quilt border; about 30 yds of black $^1/_4$"W single-fold bias tape; 4 yds of black double-fold bias tape; 36" x 36" quilt batting; paper-backed fusible web; white, green, and red quilting thread.

Cutting main quilt pieces: $^1/_4$" seams are included. **From white-on-white print** – Cut one square $12^1/_2$" x $12^1/_2$". Cut two squares $11^1/_8$" x $11^1/_8$", then cut these squares diagonally in half to make four triangles. **From print (for sashing)** – Cut four strips $1^3/_4$" x $12^1/_2$".

From solid red – Cut four squares $1^3/_4$" x $1^3/_4$". **From gold/black print** – Cut four sashing strips $1^3/_4$" x 21" and four strips $1^3/_4$" x $31^1/_2$". **From red print** – Cut eight squares $1^3/_4$" x $1^3/_4$". **From muslin** – Cut two $4^1/_2$" x $23^1/_2$" strips and two $^1/_2$" x $31^1/_2$" strips.

Making appliqué patterns: Enlarge assembly diagrams to the sizes indicated. Make individual patterns for each poinsettia petal and holly leaf. Make one pattern each for poinsettia leaf, holly berry, and poinsettia center.

Cutting appliqué motifs: Fuse web to wrong side of remaining fabrics. **From red print** – Cut one of each petal. **From green print** – Cut four of each holly leaf. **From different green-print scraps** – Cut eight poinsettia leaves. **From solid red** – Cut 12 holly berries. **From yellow** – Cut one poinsettia center.

Appliquéing motifs: Referring to assembly diagrams, arrange appliqué motifs on white-on-white square and on each triangle; fuse in place.

Assembling center panel: $^1/_4$" seams allowed. Sew a short (print) sashing strip to opposite sides of poinsettia square. Sew a solid-red square to each end of the other two print sashing strips. Sew strips to remaining sides of square. Now, sew a triangle to each side of square. Sew a 21" gold/black sashing strip to opposite sides of assembly. Sew a red print square to each end of other two 21" strips. Sew strips to remaining sides of square.

Crazy-quilt border: Sew $23^1/_2$" muslin strips to opposite sides of center panel. Sew $31^1/_2$" muslin strips to remaining sides. From the four different prints, cut irregular pieces, no wider or longer than $4^1/_4$" (see photo). Arrange pieces on muslin border until muslin is completely covered. Trim edges of pieces even with seamlines and raw edges; fuse in place.

Outer sashing: Sew two remaining gold/black strips to opposite sides of assembly, same as for other sashing strips. Sew a red-print square to each end of other two strips. Sew strips to assembly, as before.

Adding bias tape "leading": Use single-fold bias tape. Do not unfold tape or cut pieces in advance. Start at center and work out to edges of wall hanging top: Baste tape along each edge of each appliqué motif; cut tape when it meets a seamline, a raw edge of a new shape, or tape you've already basted. Always leave $^1/_4$" extra to tuck under tape. Next, baste tape to edges of sashing and crazy-quilt border, tucking under extra $^1/_4$" ends as you go. Do not outline top with tape. Secure long edges of each tape using small blindstitches. Remove basting.

Assembling quilt top: On a flat surface, place backing face down; spread batting on top of backing; lay quilt top face up on batting, edges even. Baste a large "X" through assembly (use long stitches), starting at center and stitching outward toward each corner. Next, baste rows of horizontal lines spaced 6" to 8" apart. Finish basting with a row of stitches around perimeter of assembly.

Hand quilting: Using thread to match background fabric, quilt wall hanging along each appliqué and bias tape edges. When all quilting is completed, remove basting, except the stitches around edges of the quilt.

Finishing: Trim batting to just inside quilt top and backing. Unfold one edge of double-fold bias tape; pin to top, right sides facing, along the fold (gutter) of tape, edges even; gather slightly at quilt corners for a smooth turn. Stitch along fold, then bring tape to back of quilt; slipstitch.

Optional rod pocket (for hanging): Cut a fabric strip 8¹/₂" x 33"; hem raw ends. Fold lengthwise in half, wrong sides facing; stitch long side only; turn right side out. Slipstitch sleeve to backing. Slip quilt on a curtain rod; mount rod on wal.

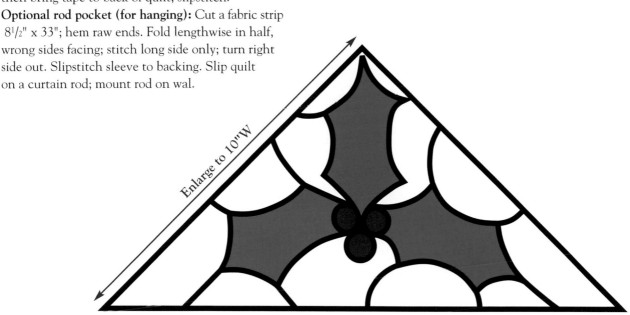

Quilt Assembly Diagrams

Enlarge to 12"W

121

PATCHWORK STAR

You need: Remnants of velvet; tailor's chalk; gold embroidery floss; fiberfill; 8 small buttons; 12" of 1"W velvet ribbon.

Cutting: Use full-size pattern to cut 16 diamond shapes from velvet; transfer marks with tailor's chalk.

Making star: *All stitching is done with ¼" seams, right sides facing and raw edges even.* Pin two diamonds together along one long edge, matching marks. Stitch one side from round to square marks; unfold. Continue adding more diamonds, alternating colors, until eight are joined. Stitch final seam to complete star front. Make star back in same way. Embroider herringbone stitches along each seam. Pin front to back, matching seams. Stitch edges, leaving opening along one edge. Trim corners; turn. Stuff; slipstitch opening closed.

Finishing: Sew a button at each outer tip. Sew ends of ribbon to back of star for hanger.

FAMILY WREATH

You need: 15" straw wreath form; crib-size quilt batting; calico remnants totaling about 2 yds; velvet remnants totaling about ½ yd; embroidery floss to contrast velvet; assorted buttons; 1 yd each of two 1"W ribbons.

Preparing wreath form: Cut batting into 3"W strips. Pin end of one strip to wreath form; wrap around form and pin end. Wrap and pin remaining strips in same way.

Embellishing: Cut calico into at least twenty 5" x 13" strips. Press under 1" on one short end of each strip. Pin and wrap strips same as for batting, overlapping ends. Embroider names on velvet as desired using three strands of floss. Cut out names, leaving fabric border around each. Turn under edges of each velvet piece; stitch to wreath with decorative stitches as desired. Sew buttons randomly to wreath.

Finishing: Tie 1"W ribbons together in a bow; stitch to top of wreath for hanging loop.

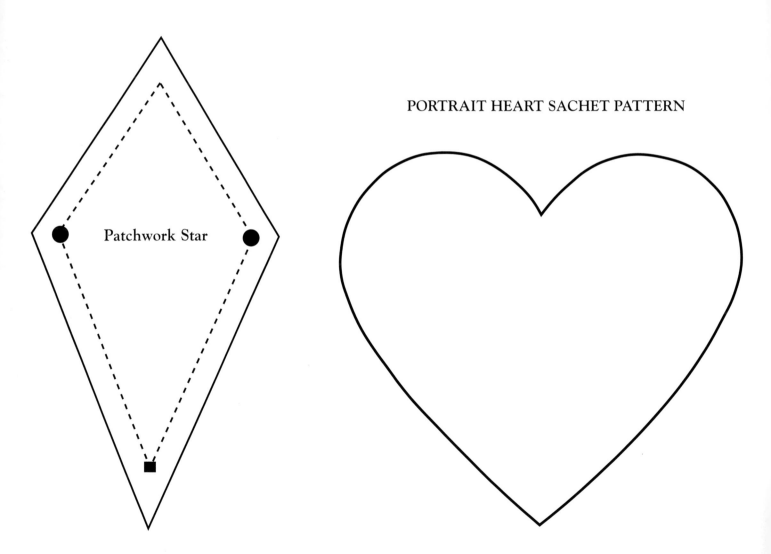

Patchwork Star

PORTRAIT HEART SACHET PATTERN

by the chimney (pages 20-25)

SCALLOPED STOCKING

You need: 1/2 yd red felt; 1/8 yd cream felt; 1/2 yd star-print fabric; red embroidery floss; 6" of red braid trim.

Cutting: Enlarge stocking pattern (page 125) to 6 1/2"W. Enlarge scalloped cuff pattern (page 125) to 12 1/2"W. *From red felt* – Cut two stocking sections. *From cream felt* – Cut one 4 1/2" x 12 1/2" cuff. *From star fabric* – Cut two stocking sections for lining and two scalloped cuff sections.

Making stocking: *All stitching is done with 1/4" seams, right sides facing and raw edges even, unless noted.* Stitch felt stocking sections together, leaving upper edge open. Clip curves; turn. Stitch lining same as stocking; do not turn. Stitch scalloped cuff sections together along scalloped edge. Clip curves and turn; press. Pin felt cuff to scalloped cuff, right sides up, with upper edges even. Using floss, stitch scallops to cream cuff with running stitches to make cuff. Fold cuff in half; stitch short end. Turn; baste to upper edge of stocking, raw edges even and right sides up. Fold braid trim in half for hanging loop; pin to stocking, over cuff, at top of back edge. Slip stocking into lining, right sides facing. Stitch upper edge, leaving 3" opening for turning. Turn lining to inside; slipstitch opening closed.

DISH TOWEL STOCKING

You need: 1 dish towel; 1/3 yd white fabric; 1/4 yd of 1/2"W ribbon; 1 small button.

Cutting: Enlarge stocking pattern (page 124) to 4 1/2"W. *From dish towel* – Cut two stocking sections. *From white fabric* – Cut two stocking (lining) sections and one 5" x 8 1/2" cuff.

Making stocking: *All stitching is done with 1/4" seams.* Pin each pair of stockings together, right sides facing. Stitch side and lower edges, leaving upper edge open. Clip curves. Turn stocking only right side out. Fold cuff in half crosswise; pin and stitch short end. Fold cuff in half, wrong sides facing and raw edges even. Baste to upper edge of stocking. Fold ribbon in half for hanging loop; pin to stocking, over cuff, at top of back edge. Slip stocking into lining, right sides facing. Stitch upper edge, leaving 3" opening for turning. Turn lining to inside; slipstitch opening closed.

Finishing: Stitch button to cuff.

TOILE STOCKING

You need: Fabrics – 1/2 yd toile, 1/2 yd gingham, 1/2 yd lining; 1 1/2 yds gingham piping.

Cutting: Enlarge stocking pattern (page 125) to 6 1/2"W. *From toile* – Cut two stocking sections and one 2" x 7" hanging loop. *From gingham* – Cut one 4" x 40" strip for pleated cuff. *From lining* – Cut two stocking sections.

Making stocking: *All stitching is done with 1/4" seams.* Pin and baste piping to side and lower edges of stocking front. Pin stocking front to back. Stitch side and lower edges, leaving upper edge open. Turn right side out.

Making pleated cuff: Fold gingham strip in half lengthwise; stitch short end. Fold in half crosswise, wrong sides facing and raw edges even; baste raw edges. Pin 1/2" pleats along raw edge. Pin pleated cuff to upper edge of stocking, right sides facing; adjust pleats to fit. Baste 1/2" from edge. Pin and baste piping over pleated cuff.

Making lining: Pin and stitch lining same as stocking.

Making hanging loop: Fold loop in half lengthwise; stitch long edge. Turn; fold in half crosswise. Pin ends to upper back corner of stocking, over cuff.

Assembling: Slip stocking into lining, right sides facing; stitch upper edge, leaving 3" opening for turning. Turn lining to inside of stocking; slipstitch opening closed. Fold down cuff.

PEPPERMINT STOCKING

You need: Wool sweaters – red, white; laundry detergent; tapestry needle; tapestry yarn – red, white; 3 white buttons.

Felting wool: Machine-wash sweaters in hot water and detergent. Repeat wash cycle several times. Dry as desired.

Cutting: Enlarge stocking pattern (page 124) to 4"W. *From red wool* – Cut two stocking sections, one 1" x 6" hanging loop, and three 1" circles. *From white wool* – Cut one 2 1/2" x 8 1/2" cuff and three 1 1/2" circles.

Making front: Sew a button in the center of each red circle. Layer red circles on white circles; sew around edges using white yarn. Sew layered circles on one stocking section using red yarn.

Making stocking: Pin front to remaining stocking section (back), wrong sides facing. Stitch sides and lower edges, leaving upper edge open. Pin and stitch short ends of cuff in 1/4" seam. Pin and stitch cuff, right side out, inside upper edge of stocking. Fold cuff to outside of stocking.

Finishing: Fold hanging loop lengthwise into thirds; stitch down center using red yarn. Fold hanging loop in half; stitch ends inside upper corner of stocking.

LACY STOCKING

You need: Knitted fabric from sweaters – red, white ribbed, white knitted-lace; 3 red buttons.

Cutting: Wash red wool several times to shrink. Enlarge stocking pattern (page 125) to 6½"W. *From red wool* – Cut two stocking sections and one 1" x 8" hanging loop. *From knitted lace* – Cut two stocking sections. *From white wool* – Cut one 3" x 12½" cuff.

Decorating: Baste lace section to each red section, right sides up, to make stocking front and back.

Making stocking: *All stitching is done with ¼" seams.* Pin and stitch front to back, right sides facing, leaving upper edge open. Turn. Pin and stitch short ends of cuff. Place cuff, right side out, inside stocking; stitch cuff to stocking. Fold cuff to outside of stocking.

Finishing: Stitch buttons to cuff. Fold hanging loop in half; stitch ends inside upper corner of stocking.

FRUITED GARLAND (continued)

Preparing: Secure garland to mantel. Make vertical cuts in lime rinds. Insert picks into center of whole fruits and pomanders. Twist wire through edges of orange slices.

Embellishing: Twist wire around picks and wires to form clusters; glue clusters into garland. Glue berry stems and stems of boxwood and pepper berries into garland. Twist ribbon around garland. Wire bows to ends of garlands.

Dish Towel Stocking – Enlarge to 4½"W
Peppermint Stocking – Enlarge to 4"W

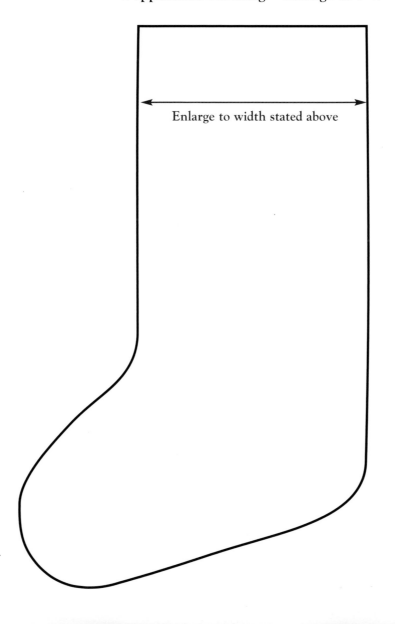

Enlarge to width stated above

Scalloped Stocking Cuff

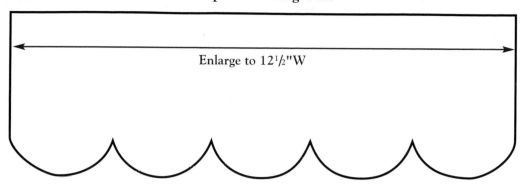

Enlarge to 12½"W

Scalloped Stocking
Toile Stocking
Lacy Stocking

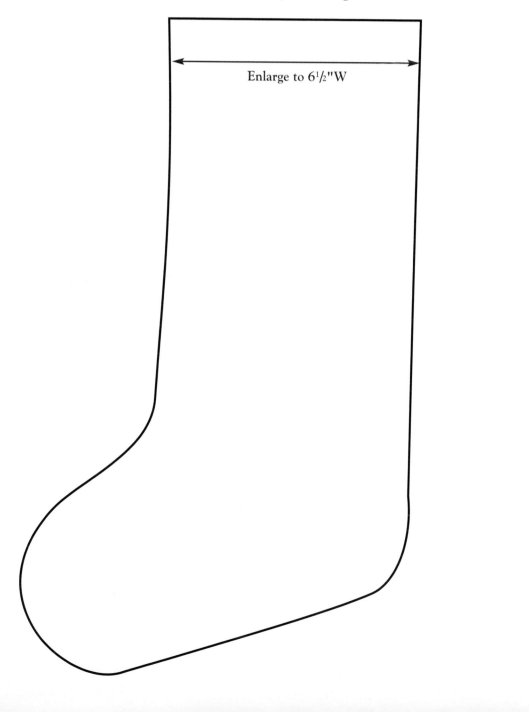

Enlarge to 6½"W

FATHER CHRISTMAS (continued)

Cutting: Enlarge patterns. From red felt, cut two body sections, two hat sections, four arm sections, and one base. From white, cut one beard. From tan, cut one face. Transfer facial features to face. From cardboard, cut one base.

Making figure: *All stitching is done with 1/4" seams, right sides facing and raw edges even, unless noted.* **Body** – Stitch body front to body back, leaving lower edge open. Turn. **Arms** – Stitch each pair of arms, leaving opening along one long edge. Turn; stuff. Slipstitch opening closed. Paint mitten with black paint on end of each arm (see photo, page 24). Cut two 3 3/4" pieces of 7/8"W gingham ribbon. Sew or glue one ribbon to each arm so it overlaps mitten. Pin arms to sides of body. Place button at top of each arm. Stitch each arm to body, through button. **Base** – Stuff body. Place cardboard base, then felt base over lower opening edge of body. Whipstitch felt base to body, covering cardboard.

Making face: Pin face and beard sections together, right sides up. Stitch close to all edges. Paint facial features with black paint. Paint eyebrows white. Paint tiny white dots in centers of eyes. Using cotton swab, apply blush to cheeks. Sew or glue face to body at upper edge.

Decorating body: Glue 5/8"W gingham ribbon down front center of body to within 1 1/2" of base. Glue 7/8"W gingham ribbon around body 1" above base. Slip one end of velvet ribbon through buckle; sew or glue end to make belt. Wrap belt around waist and insert other end through buckle. Glue belt in place.

Making hat: Fold hat in half, matching long edges. Stitch long raw edge, leaving bottom edge open. Turn. Sew or glue 5/8"W ribbon to edge of hat. Sew white pom-pom to tip.

Making tree: Cut 4" circle from tan felt. Sew running stitches along edges of circle, leaving long thread ends. Cover tree base with fiberfill. Place circle over base, pulling up thread to gather. Insert additional fiberfill, if needed. Secure thread with several small stitches. Tie twine over gathers.

Finishing: Use glue gun to glue hat on head and tree in arms.

POM-POM PILLOW

You need: 1/2 yd red felt; 12" square foam pillow form; 2 yds white ball fringe.

Cutting: Cut two 16" squares from red felt.

Assembling: Place felt squares together. Cut 1"H scallops evenly along each edge, starting at corners. Place pillow form between squares. Pin felt close to foam. Baste around edges of foam.

Finishing: Sew ball fringe to pillow through all layers along basting lines.

Father Christmas

1 square = 1"

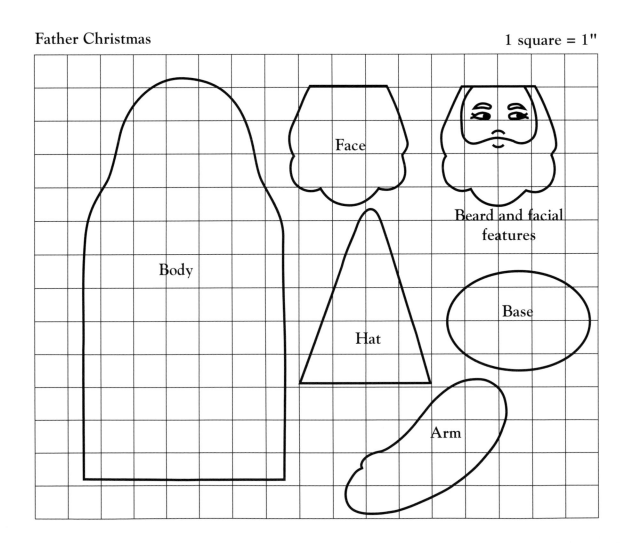

ZIGZAG PILLOW

You need: Felt – $1/2$ yd each red, camel; 12" square foam pillow form; pinking shears; 40 small jingle bells.

Cutting: Cut two 17" squares from each color of felt.

Assembling: Place red squares together. Using pinking shears, cut five 2"L triangles evenly spaced along each edge, starting at corners. Place camel squares together. Using pinking shears, cut four 2"L triangles on each edge, spacing triangles evenly between red triangles. Layer one red square, one camel square, pillow form, one camel square, and one red square. Pin felt close to form. Baste around edges of form.

Finishing: Sew a jingle bell on each side at base of each red triangle, stitching through all layers.

ONE STOCKING, SIX WAYS

You need (for all stockings): Felt – 36" x 36" piece each loden green, red, white, hunter green; white and red ball-shaped buttons; half-ball self-cover buttons – $1 1/2$", $1 1/8$", $7/8$", $3/4$"; 1 yd red jumbo rickrack; 2 yds of $5/8$"W red grosgrain ribbon.

Assembling basic stocking: Enlarge patterns (page 128). Cut out pieces as described in individual directions that follow. Sew decorations to stocking front. Pin stocking front to stocking back, right sides facing and raw edges even. Stitch side and lower edges in $1/4$" seam, leaving upper edge open. Pin and stitch short ends of cuff together in $1/4$" seam, right sides facing. Pin right side of cuff to wrong side of stocking. Stitch in $1/4$" seam. Turn stocking right side out. Turn cuff to outside of stocking.

Finishing basic stocking: Cut 8" of ribbon for hanging loop. Fold in half and stitch ends inside upper corner of stocking.

Loden stocking with white cuff and holly leaves: From loden, cut two stocking sections. From white, cut one straight cuff, one small toe, and one small heel. From red, cut one large toe and one large heel. From loden and hunter green, cut large and small holly leaves as desired. Pin large, then small toe and heel sections to stocking front. Stitch around edges of small sections. Follow basic assembling directions to assemble stocking. *Finishing* – Sew red buttons to cuff in clusters of three for berries. Sew leaves near berries. Follow basic finishing directions for hanging loop.

Red stocking with loden cuff and poinsettia: From red, cut two stocking sections and two small holly leaves. From loden, cut one straight cuff. From white, cut four large holly leaves. Arrange white leaves to form poinsettia on front of stocking.

Stitch through centers of leaves. Follow manufacturer's directions to cover $7/8$" button with loden. Sew covered button in center of poinsettia. Follow basic assembling directions to assemble stocking. *Finishing* – Sew red leaves and three white buttons to cuff. Follow basic finishing directions for hanging loop.

White stocking with hunter green cuff and flowers: From white, cut two stocking sections. From hunter green, cut one straight cuff. From red, cut three flowers, one large toe, and one large heel. Pin large, then small toe and heel sections to stocking front. Stitch around edges of small sections. Follow basic assembling directions to assemble stocking. *Finishing* – Follow manufacturer's directions to cover three $3/4$" buttons with loden. Arrange flowers on cuff; place button in center of each flower. Sew buttons to cuff through flower centers. Follow basic finishing directions for hanging loop.

Hunter-green stocking with white cuff: From hunter green, cut two stocking sections. From white, cut one large toe section, one large heel section, and one straight cuff. From loden, cut four small holly leaves. Pin toe and heel sections to stocking front. Pin rickrack along edges (see photo, page 25). Stitch through rickrack to attach toe and heel sections. Sew rickrack to cuff, 1" from upper edge. Follow basic assembling directions to assemble stocking. *Finishing* – Sew four red buttons to cuff. Sew leaves to cuff. Follow basic finishing directions for hanging loop.

Loden stocking with red cuff and tree: From loden, cut two stocking sections. From hunter green, cut one tree and two large holly leaves. From red, cut one straight cuff, one large toe, one large heel, and one rectangle slightly smaller than tree. Pin toe and heel sections to stocking front; stitch around edges. Sew rectangle to center of stocking front. Sew tree in center of rectangle. Fold cuff in half, matching short edges. Arrange holly leaves on front half of cuff. Stitch through centers of leaves. Follow basic assembling directions to assemble stocking. *Finishing* – Sew three white buttons to cuff. Follow basic finishing directions for hanging loop.

Red stocking with white scalloped cuff: From red, cut two stocking sections. From white, cut one scalloped cuff. Follow manufacturer's directions to cover 15 assorted buttons with a variety of white, hunter green, and loden remnants; sew randomly to front of stocking. Follow basic assembling directions to assemble stocking. *Finishing* – Follow basic finishing directions for hanging loop.

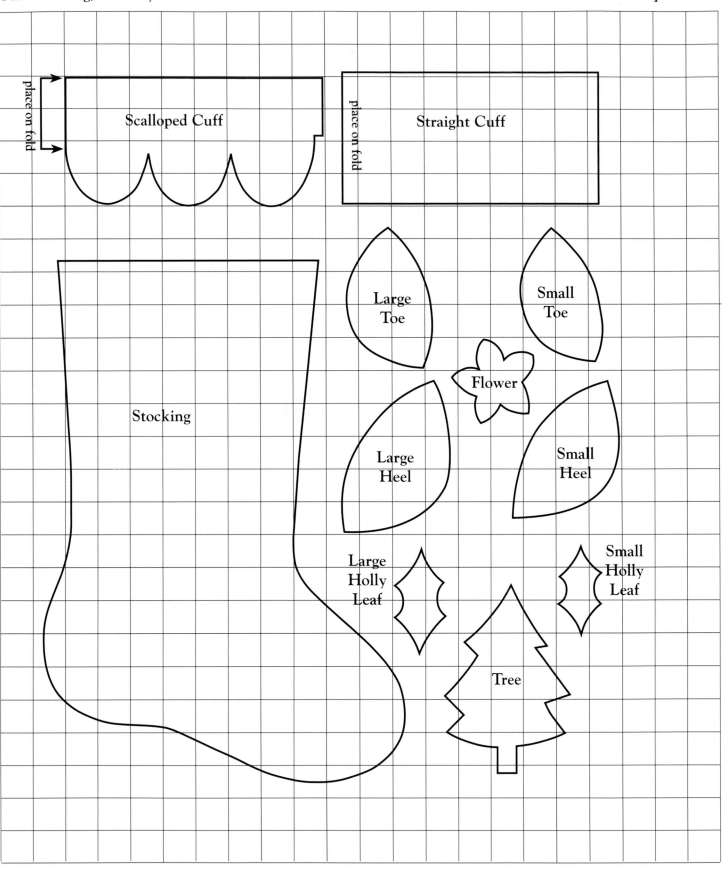

place on fold

Scalloped Cuff

place on fold

Straight Cuff

Stocking

Large
Toe

Small
Toe

Flower

Large
Heel

Small
Heel

Large
Holly
Leaf

Small
Holly
Leaf

Tree

make it merry (pages 26-29)

CHEERY CANARY

You need: Felt – one 9" x 12" rectangle each dark gold, red; 6" of black yarn; fiberfill; 2 black E beads; 12" of nylon fishing line; fabric glue.

Cutting: Use full-size patterns and cut two body sections from gold felt and two wing sections from red felt.

Assembling: For legs, knot each end of yarn. Fold yarn in half and place on top of one body piece, with fold at bottom and "legs" towards center of body. Pin body sections together with legs sandwiched between. Stitch edges, catching yarn in stitching and leaving 2" opening along upper edge. Turn; stuff. Slipstitch opening closed. Glue wings to sides of body. Sew beads to sides of head, pulling thread tight. Stitch several times through beak, pulling thread tight.

Finishing: Stitch fishing line through top of ornament; knot ends to form hanging loop.

ENVELOPE ORNAMENTS

You need (for each): Felt – 9" x 12" piece of red, scraps of tan and green; pinking shears (optional); embroidery floss in desired colors; 2/3 yd of 1/4"W red ribbon; jingle bells – 2 small, 1 medium.

Cutting: Cut one 4" x 9" piece of red felt for envelope (use pinking shears, if desired), one 1 1/4"W heart from red, one 1 3/4" x 1 1/4" piece of tan for stamp, and one 1" x 2" piece of green for address strip.

Assembling: Embroider initials or name on address strip as desired using floss. Sew heart to stamp. Fold envelope in thirds crosswise to form pocket and flap; mark folds with pins. Open out flat. Pin and stitch address strip and stamp strip to front. Fold one section against center third. Pin side edges together; stitch 1/4" from side edges to form pocket. Trim remaining flap section to a point.

Finishing: Cut ribbon in half. Stitch one piece at each upper corner of ornament. Stitch small jingle bell over end of each ribbon. Tie ribbon ends in bow to make hanging loop. Stitch medium jingle bell 1" above the spot where flap point meets envelope back. Cut corresponding slit in flap; slip bell through slit to close ornament.

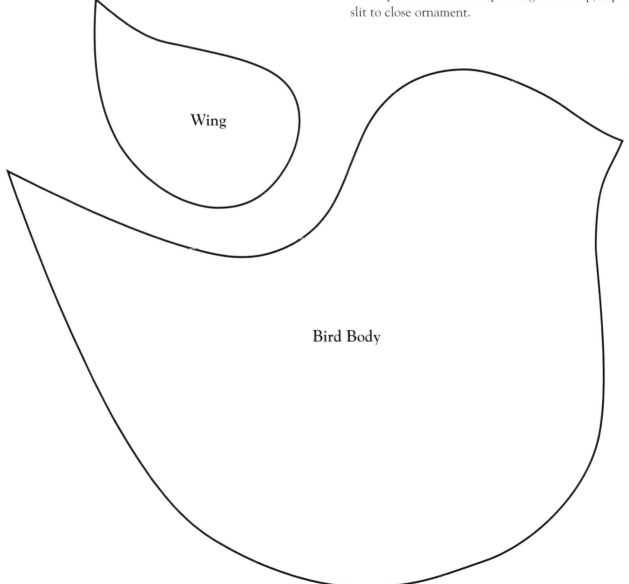

Wing

Bird Body

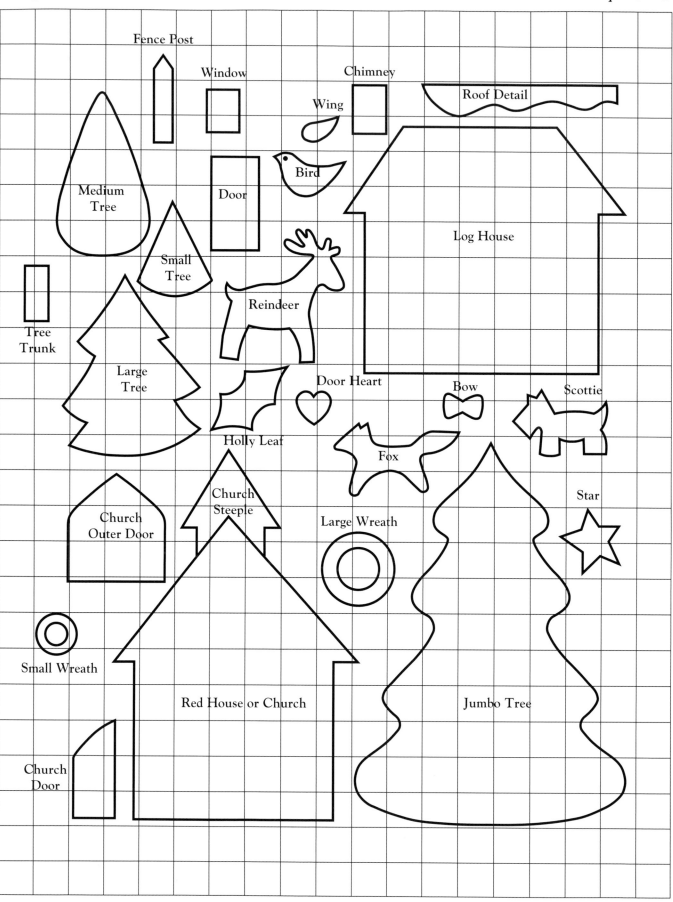

Fence Post

Window

Chimney

Wing

Roof Detail

Bird

Medium Tree

Door

Log House

Small Tree

Reindeer

Tree Trunk

Large Tree

Door Heart

Bow

Scottie

Holly Leaf

Fox

Church Outer Door

Church Steeple

Large Wreath

Star

Small Wreath

Red House or Church

Jumbo Tree

Church Door

PARTRIDGE AND PEAR WALL HANGING

You need: Felt – 28" x 38" piece light olive, 17" x 29" piece cream, 11" x 19" piece dark green, two 9" x 12" pieces red, one 9" x 12" piece each dark gold, kelly green, beige, white, brown; double-sided adhesive – sheet and 1/2"W; tailor's chalk; glue gun; 1 black E bead; large gold sequins; 1 1/2 yds of 7/8"W gold wire-edge ribbon; 20" gold curtain rod.

Making backing: Enlarge patterns. Cut 20" x 38" rectangle from light olive felt. Using pattern, cut scallops along one short edge for bottom of wall hanging. Apply strip adhesive along back of other short edge. Turn under 3" to form rod pocket. Press in place.

Embellishing: Fold dark green felt in half lengthwise. Draw a freehand half-tree shape centered on fold; cut out through both layers. Using patterns, cut pieces from remaining felt. Use strip adhesive to apply large shapes and pieces of sheet adhesive to apply small pieces to wall hanging. Glue bead to partridge for eye. Glue sequins to wall hanging. Cut 18" of ribbon; tie in bow. Glue to top of tree. Tie remaining ribbon in bow; glue to tree trunk.

Finishing: Insert rod through pocket; hang as desired.

Partridge and Pear Wall Hanging

1 square = 1"

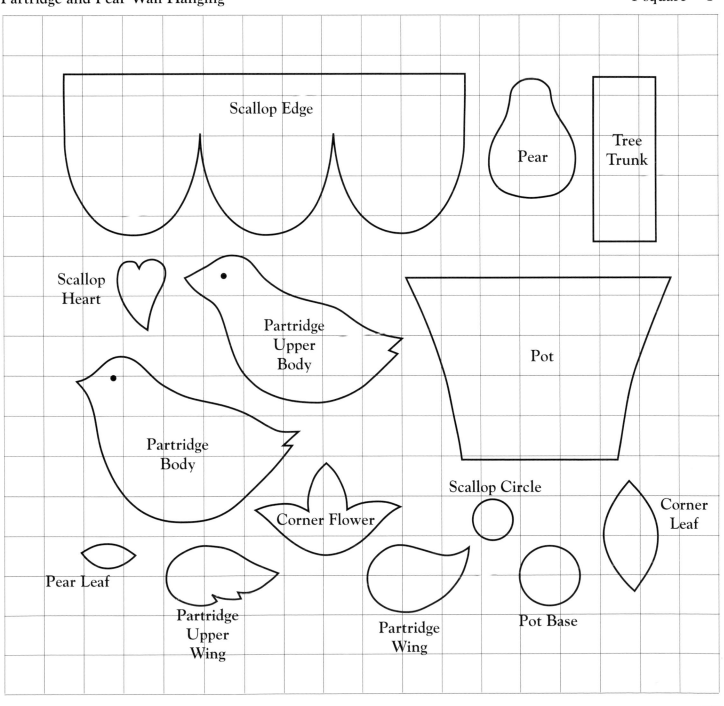

133

MR. AND MRS. TEDDY BEAR CLAUS (continued)

For Mr. Claus – Stitch hook-and-loop tape inside front edges of coat.

Assembling skirt: Stitch short edges of plaid wool together. Turn lower edge under 1/2"; stitch near fold to hem. Turn upper edge under 1/2"; stitch near raw edge to form casing, leaving opening. Cut 12" of elastic; insert through casing. Stitch ends of elastic together; finish stitching casing.

Assembling pants: Turn under 1/2" on edge of each pants leg; stitch near fold to hem. Fold each pants section in half lengthwise; stitch inner leg seam. Stitch pants sections together at crotch seam, matching leg seams. Turn. Turn under 1/2" on waist edge; stitch near raw edge to form casing, leaving opening. Cut 12" of elastic; insert through casing. Stitch ends of elastic together; finish stitching casing.

Assembling Mr. Claus's hat: Cut openings where marked in one hat section. Turn under raw edges of openings; stitch near folds. Stitch hat sections together, leaving lower (straight) edge open. Turn. Place on head to determine ear placement. Remove hat; slipstitch ears to head same as for Mrs. Claus.

Trimming: Cut white felt into 3"W strips. Fold strips in half widthwise; stitch near long edge to form trim. Turn; fold strips so seams are centered. Glue trim around cuffs of each coat. Glue trim around edge of Mrs. Claus's hood. Glue trim along one front edge and bottom edge of Mr. Claus's coat and around lower edge of hat.

Finishing: Cut ribbon into two equal pieces. Stitch one piece near each front neck edge at hood seam. Glue large pom-pom to Mr. Claus's hat and small pom-poms to Mrs. Claus's hood and coat. Place clothing on bears.

TARTAN ELF (continued)

Glue prairie-point trim around top of lid so points drop over edge. Glue head to body.

Making legs: Cover large box and lid with remaining tartan. Glue lid on box; glue head and body on top. Continue to paint suspenders down lid rim, ends in points. Paint two black shoes (half-circles) at bottom of box. Tie red thread through buttons; glue to ends of suspenders.

CANDY CANE SANTA

You need: Set of 5 graduated-size hexagonal Kraft paper boxes; wood trims – one 2 5/8" star, two 1 1/2" stars, two 1 1/2" circles, one 1" knob, one 2" square; paintbrushes – foam, 1/2" flat, #1 liner; primer; sandpaper; acrylic paints – red, blush, black, gold, white; glue gun; 1/4 yd muslin; 18" of 20-gauge wire; awl; 1 pair doll eyeglasses; palette knife; snow medium.

Preparing pieces: Prime boxes, lids, and all wood pieces. Sand wood pieces.

Labeling boxes and lids: Smallest to largest – #1 (Hat); #2 (Head); #3 (Chest); #4 (Waist); #5 (Tummy).

Base coating: *Red* – Boxes #1, #3, #4, #5; lid #5. *Blush* – Box #2. *Black* – Lid #4, wood square. *White* – Lids (tops only) #1, #2, #3. *Gold* – All stars; buckle details on black wood square.

Decorating box #1: Glue large gold star to box. Paint "HO HO HO!" in black with liner brush.

Decorating box #2: *Face* – Paint wood circles (cheeks) with a mixture of blush and red. Add a dab more red; paint knob (nose). Using flat brush, paint red on upper portion of cheeks; let dry. Highlight cheeks and nose with white. Glue on cheeks and nose. With liner brush paint eyes with black and add white star-shaped highlights. Let dry. *Beard and hair* – Tear muslin into 3/4"W strips. *Beard* – Cut several strips into 12" lengths until you have 29 pieces. Fold strips in half over wire; knot, letting strip ends fall evenly. *To attach beard and glasses* – Poke a hole in each side of box (where ears would be). Push ends of wire through loops in arms of glasses; push wire through poked holes, then twist wire ends inside box to secure. *Hair* – Cut remaining strips into 4"L pieces. Glue one end of each inside box (around "head"); flip strips of hair to the outside of the box. Trim bangs.

Adding "fur" trim: Stack boxes #4 and #5. Mark a 2"W band around bottom of box #5. Mark a 2 3/4"W stripe down center of boxes #4 and #5 and lid #5. With palette knife, apply snow to marked areas and rims of lids #1, #2, and #3. While snow is still wet, embed stars in "fur" trim.

Adding buckle: Glue painted wood buckle to black rim.

Finishing: Stack all boxes as shown. Set box #1 (hat) in its own lid. Fill with candy canes.

FUN FELT GIFT BAGS

You need (for each): Felt – two 9" x 12" pieces (bag), assorted remnants (reindeer or Santa ornament); black embroidery floss; ½ yd each of assorted ribbons; fiberfill; fabric glue; pinking shears; safety pin.

Making Santa: *Cutting* – Use full-size Santa patterns to cut two background pieces and one each of remaining pieces from felt remnants. ***Embroidering*** – *Use three strands of floss unless noted.* Glue all Santa pieces to one background piece. Work running stitch along head and hat. Work blanket stitch along mustache. Work onc large "X" on star. Use six strands and work two French knots for eyes. ***Assembling*** – Place background pieces together and work blanket stitch around edges, leaving an opening. Stuff with fiberfill and continue stitching to close.

Making reindeer: *Cutting* – Use full-size reindeer patterns (page 138) to cut two background pieces and one each of remaining pieces from felt remnants. ***Embroidering*** – *Use three strands of floss unless noted.* Glue all reindeer pieces to one background piece. Work running stitch along edges of head and nose; work three small stitches below nose. Work blanket stitch around muzzle and antlers. Use six strands and work two French knots for eyes. ***Assembling*** – Place background pieces together and work blanket stitch around edges, leaving an opening. Stuff with fiberfill and continue stitching to close.

Making bag: Place 9" x 12" felt pieces together. Work running stitch along side and bottom edges. Use pinking shears to trim all edges of bag. Leaving top edge open, work running stitch along top edge.

Finishing: Place gift in bag. Tie ribbons in a bow around bag. Pin ornament to bag.

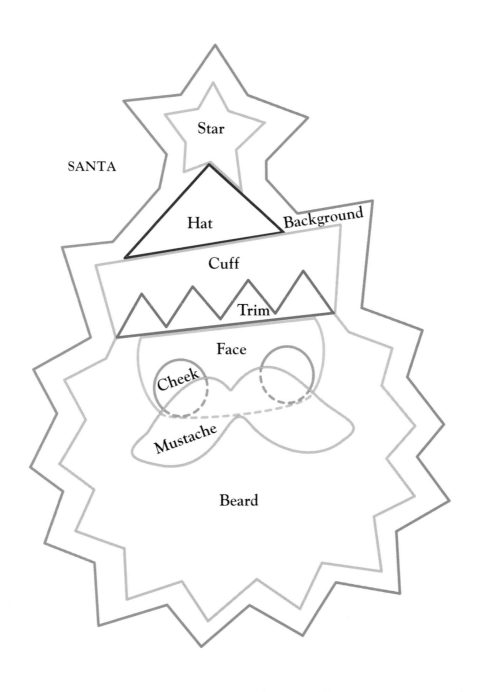

CROSSED TREBLES AFGHAN

Size: approx. 51" x 68"

You need: Worsted weight yarn – 54 ounces, (1,530 grams, 3,550 yards); crochet hook, size I (5.50 mm) or size needed for gauge.

Gauge: 7 Cross Sts and Rows 1-8 = 4"

Note: Each row is worked across length of afghan.

Stitches: Cross St – Skip next st, tr in next st, working *around* tr just made, tr in skipped st (*Figs. 1a & b*). **Cluster** – ★ YO, insert hook in st indicated, YO and pull up a loop, YO and draw through 2 loops on hook; repeat from ★ 4 times *more*, YO and draw through all 6 loops on hook (*Figs. 2a & b*). Push Cluster to *right side*.

Fig. 1a

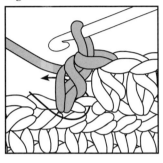

Fig. 1b

Fig. 2a

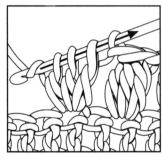

Fig. 2b

REINDEER

Body: Ch 237 *loosely*. **Row 1:** Sc in second ch from hook and in each ch across: 236 sc. **Row 2 (Right side):** Ch 4 (*counts as first tr, now and throughout*), turn; work Cross Sts across to last sc, tr in last sc: 117 Cross Sts. **Row 3:** Ch 1, turn; sc in first tr, ch 1, ★ skip next Cross St, sc in sp before next Cross St, ch 1; repeat from ★ across to last Cross St, skip last Cross St, sc in sp before last tr, sc in last tr: 236 sts. **Row 4:** Ch 4, turn; work Cross Sts across to last sc working in sc and in chs, tr in last sc: 117 Cross Sts. **Rows 5-17:** Repeat Rows 3 and 4, 6 times, then repeat Row 3 once *more*. **Rows 18-20:** Ch 1, turn, sc in each st across: 236 sc. **Row 21:** Ch 1, turn; sc in first 4 sc, work Cluster in next sc, (sc in next 5 sc, work Cluster in next sc) across to last 3 sc, sc in last 3 sc: 39 Clusters. **Row 22:** Ch 3 (*counts as first dc, now and throughout*), turn; dc in next sc and in each st across: 236 dc. **Row 23:** Ch 1, turn; sc in first 7 dc, work Cluster in next dc, (sc in next 5 dc, work Cluster in next dc) across to last 6 dc, sc in last 6 dc: 38 Clusters. **Row 24:** Ch 3, turn; dc in next sc and in each st across. **Row 25:** Ch 1, turn; sc in each dc across. **Rows 26-113:** Repeat Rows 2-25, 3 times, then repeat Rows 2-17 once *more*. Finish off.

Fringe: For each knot, cut six 15" lengths of yarn; fold in half. With *wrong* side facing, use a crochet hook to draw folded end up through a row and pull loose ends through the folded end. Pull knot tight. Spacing evenly, attach fringe across ends of rows on each end of afghan.

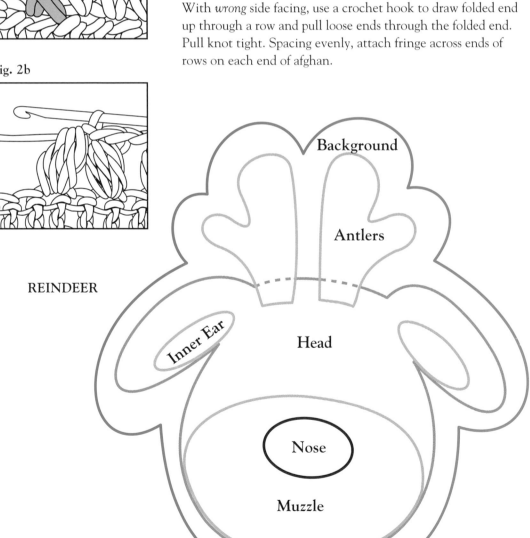

FLEECY FROSTY

You need: Polar fleece – ¹/₂ yard cream and remnants of green, yellow, and red; 4" square orange mini-print fabric; black felt remnant; ³/₄" x 8" piece of cardboard; fiberfill; skein of yellow tapestry yarn; five ¹/₂" and four ¹/₄" round black shank buttons.

Cutting: Enlarge patterns. *From cream fleece* – Cut two body sections and one base. *From green fleece* – Cut four mittens. *From yellow fleece* – Cut one 4" x 8" strip for scarf. *From red fleece* – Cut one 4" x 8" hat and two 2" x 4" scarf stripes. *From orange fabric* – Cut two 1"W x 2"H triangles for nose. *From black felt* – Cut one 2" x 8" arm section.

Assembling: *All stitching is done with ¹/₄" seams, right sides facing, unless noted.* **Mittens** – Stitch together in pairs, leaving straight edges open; trim seams. Do not turn. **Arms** – Fold arm section in half lengthwise; stitch long edges together. Insert cardboard into tube; cut in half to make two arms. Insert one arm into open end of each mitten; stitch along open edge to secure. **Body** – Pin arms to sides of body front. Pin body front to back; stitch long curved edges, leaving bottom open; also leave small opening along one side. Stitch base section to bottom opening. Clip curves; turn. Stuff firmly; slipstitch opening closed. **Nose** – Stitch nose sections together, leaving short edge open. Trim seams; turn. Stuff. Hand stitch nose to head. **Hat** – Fold fleece in half, matching short edges. Pin and stitch side and upper edge; turn. Fold up cuff at lower edge; place on head. **Scarf** – Trim 1¹/₂" off each end of scarf. Sitch red stripes to ends of scarf, then reattach the trimmed yellow pieces to make striped scarf. Trim edges neatly so scarf is 3"W. Sew yarn fringe to scarf ends; tie around snowman's neck.

Finishing: Sew on large buttons for eyes and buttons; sew on small buttons for mouth.

Fleecy Frosty

1 square = 1"

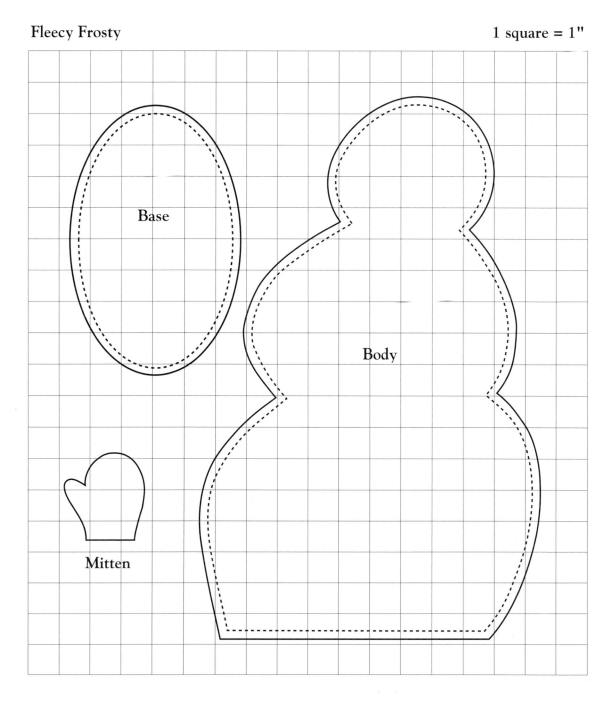

Base

Body

Mitten

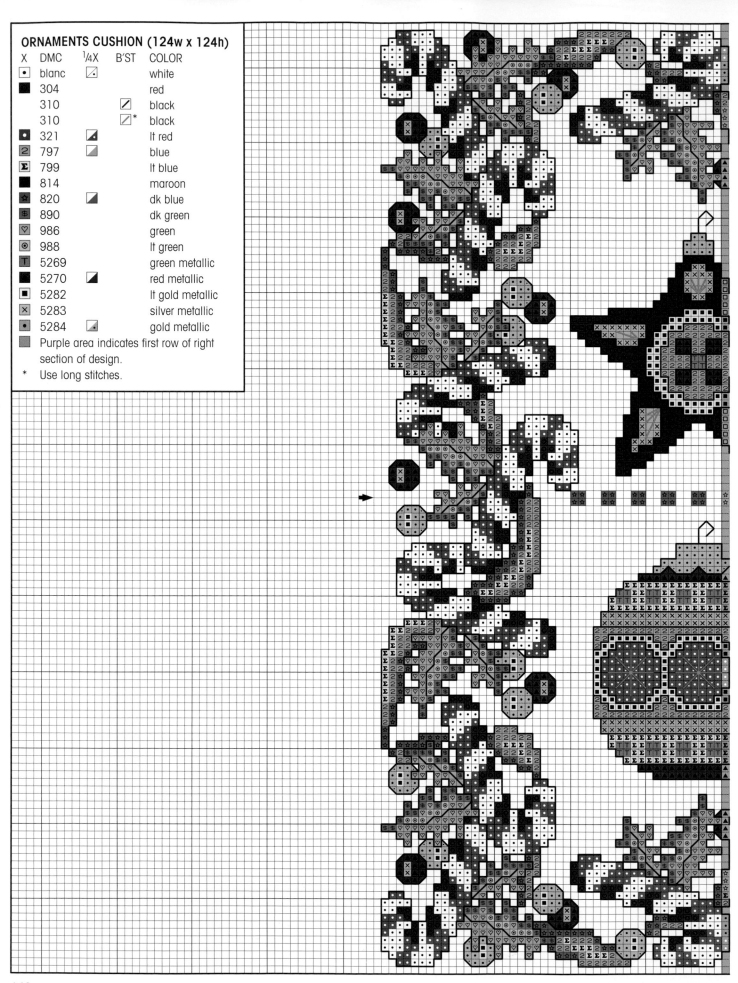

ORNAMENTS CUSHION (124w x 124h)

X	DMC	¼X	B'ST	COLOR
•	blanc			white
■	304			red
	310		◿	black
	310		◿*	black
▣	321	◿		lt red
2	797	◿		blue
Σ	799			lt blue
■	814			maroon
★	820	◿		dk blue
$	890			dk green
♡	986			green
⊙	988			lt green
T	5269			green metallic
■	5270	◿		red metallic
▪	5282			lt gold metallic
✕	5283			silver metallic
•	5284	◿		gold metallic

Purple area indicates first row of right section of design.

* Use long stitches.

140

BUTTONS AND BOWS CARDIGAN

You need: Cardigan; assorted ribbons; assorted buttons.
To do: Tie ribbons into bows. Sew buttons and bows to cardigan.

CREST CARDIGAN

You need: Cardigan; crest appliqué; gold cord trim.
To do: Sew crest to cardigan. Beginning several inches from one end of cord at bottom of crest, sew cord along edges of crest. Knot ends of cord together at bottom of crest. Trim cord ends to 1". Unravel cord ends.

ORNAMENTS CARDIGAN

You need: Cardigan; 2 Christmas-print fabric scraps; paper-backed fusible web; 6" of 1/2"W metallic trim; 2 gold buttons; metallic gold rickrack; gold thread.
To do: Trace full-size ornament patterns onto paper side of web. Fuse web to fabrics; cut out ornaments. Fuse ornaments to cardigan. Sew rickrack to cardigan from shoulder seam to tops of ornaments. Using gold thread and a medium machine-satin stitch, sew over raw edges of ornaments. Sew short pieces of metallic trim to top of ornaments for ornament caps. Sew buttons to ornament caps.

CHERRIES CARDIGAN

You need: Cardigan; 1" red pom-poms; fabric glue; green felt; green embroidery floss; brown yarn.
To do: Use full-size leaf pattern to cut pairs of leaves from felt. Glue pom-poms (for cherries) and leaves to cardigan. Work green running stitches down center of each leaf. Sew brown yarn between pom-poms and leaves to resemble stems.

SNOWMAN SWEATER

You need: Crewneck sweater; scraps of white felt and plaid fabric; embroidery floss – white, black, orange.
To do: Use full-size snowman pattern to cut snowman from felt. *Use three strands of floss for stitching.* To secure snowman to sweater, work white blanket stitches around snowman edges. Work white outline stitches for arms, orange satin stitches for nose, and black French knots for eyes and mouth. For scarf, cut a 1/4" x 6" plaid strip; knot center. Stitch knot to snowman; trim ends.

HOBO PATCH SWEATER

You need: Crewneck sweater; scraps of plaid fabrics; paper-backed fusible web; embroidery floss.
To do: Fuse web to wrong sides of fabrics. Cut squares of various sizes from fabric. Fuse squares to sweater. Use six strands of floss to whipstitch around edges of squares.

TARTAN BUTTON SWEATER

You need: Mock turtleneck sweater; 1 1/4" buttons to cover with fabric; scraps of tartan fabric; 12" lengths of 1 1/4"W wire-edge tartan ribbons; glue gun; safety pins.
To do: Follow manufacturer's instructions to cover each button with fabric. Pull ends of wire on one edge of each ribbon to gather ribbon into a circle; glue to button back. Pin buttons to sweater.

STARS AND BUTTONS CARDIGAN

You need: Cardigan; assorted gold buttons; gold star appliqués.
To do: Replace buttons. Sew additional buttons and appliqués to cardigan.

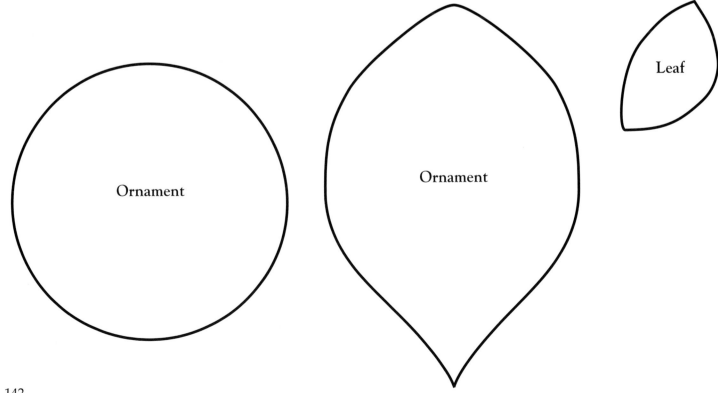

Ornament

Ornament

Leaf

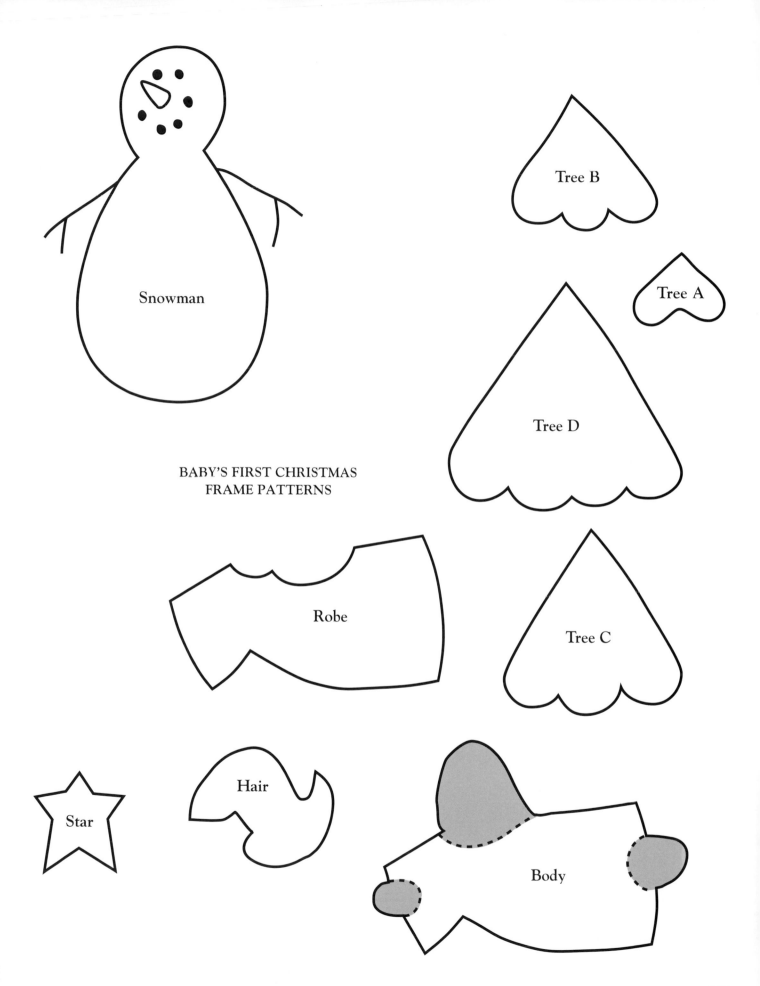

Snowman

Tree B

Tree A

Tree D

BABY'S FIRST CHRISTMAS
FRAME PATTERNS

Robe

Tree C

Star

Hair

Body

ELF PUPPETS (continued)

black; black fine-point permanent marker; 7mm pom-poms –
1 beige, 10 yellow, 4 green, 2 red.

Cutting: Enlarge patterns. Cut out following felt pieces: ***Front-facing elf*** – two yellow bodies, two red hats, two each light tan hands and ears, one light tan face, two pink cheeks, one green pants, two green suspenders. ***Side-facing elf*** – two red bodies, two green hats, one each cream face and ear, two cream hands, one pink cheek.

Assembling: Stitch each body front to corresponding body back using ¼" seams, leaving bottom open. Glue ears to front of front-facing elf. Glue face, cheeks, and hands on front of each elf; glue remaining ear to side-facing elf. Glue yarn over top of head for hair. Using marker, draw eyes and mouth. Glue one hat to front of head; glue remaining hat to back of head, aligning edges. For front-facing elf, glue pants and suspenders to body. Glue pom-poms to each elf.

Elf Puppets

1 square = 1"

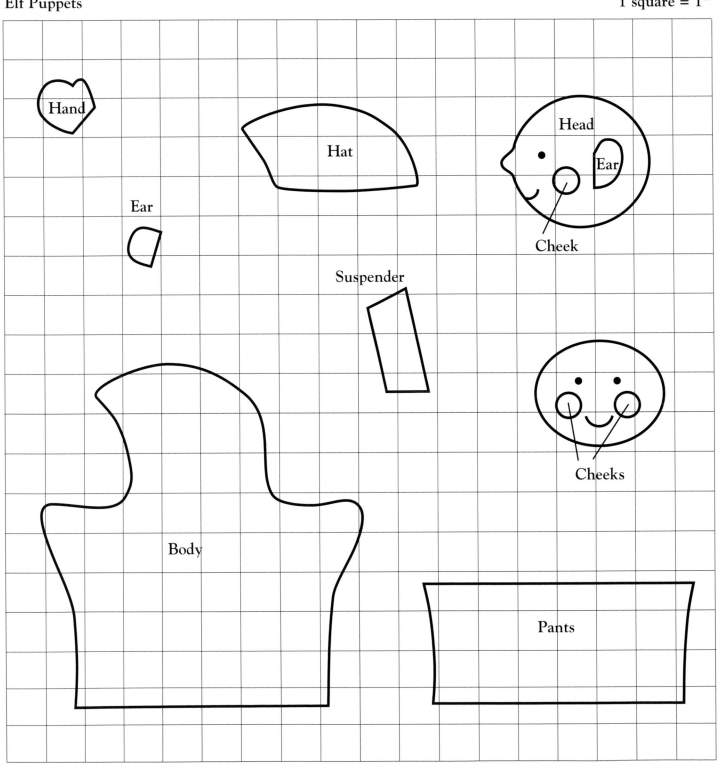

SWEET NOEL BASKET (continued)

Place on wire rack to cool. Paint eyes, buttons, and hearts.

Making pillow: Center and stitch design on one piece of fabric, using two strands of floss for cross stitches and two for backstitches. Using two strands of floss and leaving a small opening, stitch fabric pieces together eight fabric threads from edges of design. Lightly stuff pillow. Stitch final closure. Trim pillow five fabric threads from stitched line. Unravel fabric to stitched line. Cut ribbon in half. Glue one end of each ribbon to top back corner of pillow.

Decorating: Glue ginger boys and greenery in basket. Tie raffia in a bow and glue to basket. Glue ends of ribbon pieces on pillow to ginger boy's hands.

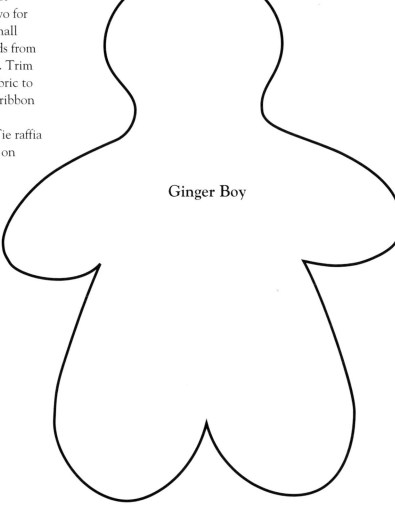

Ginger Boy

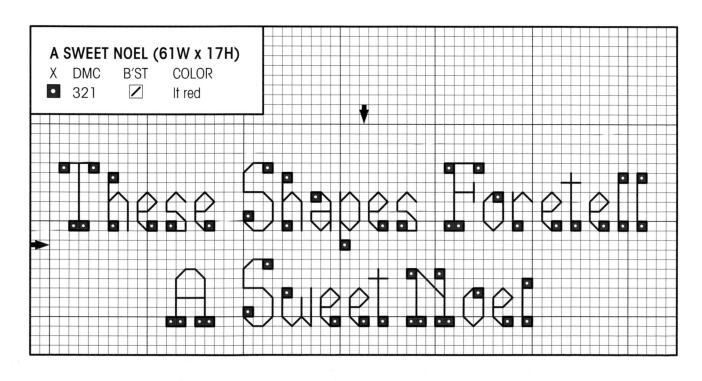

A SWEET NOEL (61W x 17H)

X	DMC	B'ST	COLOR
⊡	321	╱	lt red

GINGER DOLL

You need: Worsted weight yarn – brown (8¾ ounces, 250 grams, 550 yards), red (3½ ounces, 100 grams, 220 yards), white (1¾ ounces, 50 grams, 110 yards), green (1¾ ounces, 50 grams, 110 yards); knitting needles – regular size 6, dp size 6; stitch holder; yarn needle; fiberfill; buttons – two ⅝" matte black shank, four ½" white, two ¾" blue; 1 yd of ⅞"W yellow grosgrain ribbon; sewing needle.

Gauge: 17 sts and 24 rows in St st = 4" square; adjust needle size to achieve gauge.

Head: With dp needles and brown, cast on 50 sts, divided evenly among 3 needles. K 1 rnd. **Rnds 1 and 2:** (k14, p1, k9, p1) twice. **Rnd 3:** (k1, inc, k10, inc, k1, p1, k9, p1) twice – 54 sts. **Rnd 4:** (k16, p1, k9, p1) twice. **Rnd 5:** (k1, inc, k12, inc, k1, p1, k9, p1) twice – 58 sts. **Rnd 6:** (k1, inc, k14, inc, k1, p1, k9, p1) twice – 62 sts. **Rnd 7:** (k1, inc, k16, inc, k1, p1, k9, p1) twice – 66 sts. **Rnd 8:** (k22, p1, k9, p1) twice. **Rnd 9:** (k1, inc, k18, inc, k1, p1, k9, p1) twice – 70 sts. **Rnds 10 and 11:** (k24, p1, k9, p1) twice. **Rnd 12:** (k1, inc, k20, inc, k1, p1, k9, p1) twice – 74 sts. **Rnds 13-15:** (k26, p1, k9, p1) twice. **Rnd 16:** (k1, inc, k22, inc, k1, p1, k9, p1) twice – 78 sts. **Rnds 17-20:** (k28, p1, k9, p1) twice. **Rnd 21:** (k1, skp, k22, k2 tog, k1, p1, k9, p1) twice – 74 sts. **Rnds 22-24:** (k26, p1, k9, p1) twice. **Rnd 25:** (k1, skp, k20, k2 tog, k1, p1, k9, p1) twice – 70 sts. **Rnds 26 and 27:** (k24, p1, k9, p1) twice. **Rnd 28:** (k1, skp, k18, k2 tog, k1, p1, k9, p1) twice – 66 sts. **Rnd 29:** (k22, p1, k9, p1) twice. **Rnd 30:** (k1, skp, k16, k2 tog, k1, p1, k9, p1) twice – 62 sts. **Rnd 31:** (k1, skp, k14, k2 tog, k1, p1, k9, p1) twice – 58 sts. **Rnd 32:** (k1, skp, k12, k2 tog, k1, p1, k9, p1) twice – 54 sts. **Rnd 33:** (k16, p1, k9, p1) twice. **Rnd 34:** Bind off 16 sts, k11 and slip onto holder, bind off 16 sts, k11, turn. **Head extension:** Work in St st for 3½"; weave these 11 sts together with 11 sts on holder to make seam. Using yarn needle, sew top of extension to upper edge of front and back of head. Stuff head.

Body: Starting at bottom with dp needles and brown, cast on 88 sts, divided evenly among 3 needles. **Rnd 1:** (k9, p1, k33, p1) twice. Repeat Rnd 1 until piece measures 9" from beg. **Next rnd (shoulder extensions):** K9, p 1, k44, k11, turn. Work back and forth on 11 sts in St st for 10 rows; bind off these 11 sts. Join new sk of yarn and bind off next 33 sts. Work 11 sts in St st for 10 rows; bind off these 11 sts. Bind off rem 33 sts. Sew each edge of extensions to front and back upper edges of body. Sew head to top of body; stuff body lightly (do not sew closed).

Legs: Left leg: Turn body upside down. With brown and dp needles, cast on 10 sts. From r/s of body, pick up 1 st in center front of lower edge of body and 1 st in each of next 16 body sts, pick up st in p st and in next 9 sts, pick up st in p st and in next 16 sts; join – 54 sts. **Rnd 1:** (p1, k9, p1, k16) twice. Work 6 rnds even as established. **Next rnd (shaping rnd):** P1, k9, p1, skp, k13, inc, p1, k9, p1, inc, k13, k2 tog. Work 3 rnds even as

established. Repeat these last 4 rnds once. (Work shaping rnd and 5 rnds even as established) twice. (Work shaping rnd and 7 rnds even as established) 3 times. **Shaping foot (work back and forth in St st):** At end of last rnd turn; p 16 (Row 1 of chart); turn. **Next row (r/s):** Cast on 2 sts at beg of row and k to end. P 1 row. **Next row:** (Cast on 3 sts at beg of next row and k to end of row; p 1 row; cast on 2 sts at beg of next row; p 1 row) twice, at the same time, dec 1 st at end of first and last r/s row. Work 2 rows even. Dec 1 at beg of next r/s row. Bind off 6 sts at beg of next w/s row 3 times, at the same time, dec 1 at beg of 4th r/s row. Fasten off. Repeat for front of foot, reversing shaping. Pick up 11 side sts and work back and forth in St st until side extension reaches around entire edge of foot to end of panel. Stuff leg. Weave edge sts tog same as for head. Sew extension to front and back edges of foot. **Right leg:** Make same as Left Leg, reversing shaping.

Leg Shaping

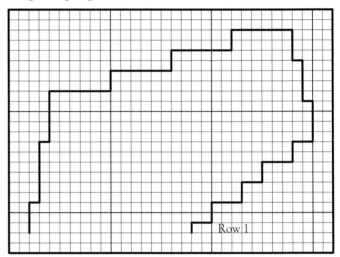

Row 1

Arms (make 2): With dp needles and brown, cast on 36 sts, divided evenly among 3 needles. K1 rnd. **Next 2 rnds:** (p1, k3, p1, k13) twice. **Next rnd:** (p1, inc, k1, inc, p1, k13) twice – 40 sts. Work 4 rnds even. **Next rnd:** (p1, inc, k3, inc, p1, k13) twice – 44 sts. Work 4 rnds even. **Next rnd:** (p1, inc, k5, inc, p1, k13) twice – 48 sts. Work 7 rnds even. **Next rnd:** (p1, k9, p1, skp, k9, k2 tog) twice – 44 sts. Work 6 rnds even. **Next rnd:** (p1, k9, p1, skp, k7, k2 tog) twice – 40 sts. Work 6 rnds even. **Next rnd:** (p1, skp, k5, k2 tog, p1, k9) twice – 36 sts. Work 1 rnd even. **Next rnd:** (p1, k7, p1, inc, k7, inc) twice – 40 sts. Work 1 rnd even. **Next rnd:** (p1, k9, p1, inc, k9, inc) twice – 44 sts. Work 11 rnds even. **Next rnd:** (p1, k7, p1, skp, k9, k2 tog) twice – 40 sts. Work 1 rnd even. **Next rnd:** (p1, k7, p1, skp, k7, k2 tog) twice – 36 sts. Work 1 rnd even. **Next rnd:** (p1, k7, p1, bind off 9) twice. Leave first 9 of rem sts on separate needle; work even on rem 9 sts until extension fits around hand to end of side panel. Weave these sts to 9 sts on separate needle same as for head. Sew side panel to front and back edges of arm. Stuff; sew arms to sides of body.

Shirt: *Shirt back:* With regular needles and red, cast on 55 sts. P 1 row. Next row (r/s): K1, (p1, k1) across. P 1 row. Repeat last 2 rows twice, then continue in St st until 4¹/₂" long from beg. Bind off 4 sts at beg of next 2 rows – 47 sts. Work even until 9" long from beg. Bind off. *Front:* With regular needles and red, cast on 55 sts. P 1 row. *Next row (r/s):* K1, (p1, k1) across. P 1 row. Repeat last 2 rows twice, then continue in St st until 4¹/₂" long from beg. Bind off 4 sts at beg of next 2 rows – 47 sts. Work even until 8" long from beg. *Shaping neck:* K12, bind off next 23 sts, k12. Dec 1 on each shoulder on next r/s row. Work even until 9" long from beg. Bind off rem 11 sts on each shoulder. *Neck edging:* Sew right shoulder seam. From r/s, with regular needles and white, pick up 37 sts evenly spaced along front neck edge and 27 sts evenly spaced along back neck edge, leaving last 10 sts open for left shoulder seam. Work 1 row St st, 4 rows rev St st; bind off. Sew left shoulder seam and neck edging seam. *Sleeves:* From r/s, with regular needles and red, pick up 45 sts evenly spaced along armhole edge. Work even in St st for 3", ending with r/s row. *Next row:* Change to white; p 1 row. *Next row (r/s):* K1, (p1, k1) across. Repeat last 2 rows twice. Bind off in k on r/s row. Sew side and sleeve seams. Sew white buttons to front of shirt, starting 2" above lower edge.

Pants front and back (make 2): With regular needles and white, cast on 55 sts. P 1 row. Work in patt same as for shirt for 6 rows. *Next row:* Change to green. K1, skp, k to last 3 sts, k2 tog, k1 (dec patt row) – 53 sts. Work 7 rows even. *Next row:* Work dec patt row same as before – 51 sts. (Work 5 rows even, work dec patt row) 3 times – 45 sts. Change to white; work in patt for 7 rows. Bind off in k on r/s row. Beg at lower edge, sew side seams for 2" on each piece (inner legs). Sew together, matching inner leg seams.

Finishing: Dress doll, tucking in shirt. Cut ribbon in half for straps. Sew one end of each strap inside front of pants; cross straps in back and sew ends inside back of pants. Sew blue buttons to front of pants at strap ends. Sew black buttons to face for eyes. Stitch mouth with red yarn and outline sts.

STUFFED GINGER PAL

You need: 16" x 30" brown wool suiting fabric; 5¹/₂" x 15¹/₂" red flannel; fiberfill; embroidery floss – red, white; felt – 30" x 2" cream strip, 30" x 1¹/₂" green strip, green scraps; pinking shears; 1 package white rickrack; fabric glue.

Cutting: Enlarge pattern. From brown fabric, cut two body sections.

Sewing: *All stitching is done with ¹/₄" seams, right sides facing and raw edges even.* **Body** – Stitch body sections together, leaving small opening. Clip curves; turn. Stuff with fiberfill; stitch opening closed. Sew gathering stitches around doll's neck; pull threads to gather neck slightly. Make several small stitches to secure gathers. **Scarf** – Overlap long edges of cream and green felt strips; stitch with large running stitches using red floss.

Hat – Fold hat fabric in half crosswise; stitch short end to make hat. Sew gathering stitches around one end of hat; pull threads to gather tightly. Secure gathers with several small stitches. Turn. Trim lower edge of hat with pinking shears; fold up ³/₄" cuff on lower edge. Cut several ¹/₂" x 2¹/₂" strips from felt scraps. Thread needle with floss; knot one end. Thread strips onto floss. Push strips to end of floss; make several small stitches through strips to form pom-pom. Sew pom-pom to top of hat.

Finishing: Use white floss to work outline stitch for mouth and satin stitches for eyes. Hand stitch rickrack around arms and legs, near lower edges. Glue hat on head. Tie scarf around neck.

Stuffed Ginger Pal 1 square = 1"

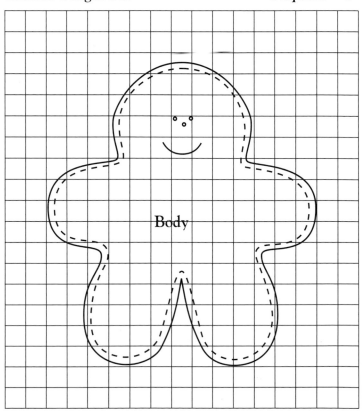

Body

GINGER KIDS

You need (for each kid): 7" x 12" piece of brown cotton or corduroy fabric; fabric glue; fiberfill; felt remnants; pinking shears (optional); embroidery floss in assorted colors; rickrack (optional); three 1/4" buttons (optional).

Making kid: *Cutting* – Use full-size pattern and cut two body sections from brown fabric. ***Sewing*** – *All stitching is done with 1/4" seams, right sides facing and raw edges even.* Stitch body sections together, leaving small opening. Clip curves; turn. ***Finishing*** – Stuff with fiberfill; stitch opening closed. Use white floss to work outline stitch for mouth and satin stitches for eyes. If desired, glue rickrack to kid.

Making vest: Use full-size pattern and cut vest from felt remnant. Trim edges with pinking shears, or use floss to stitch blanket stitches along front edges. If desired, sew buttons along one front edge of vest. If desired, cut two 1/2" square pockets for vest; trim lower corners in curves. Glue to vest front.

Making optional hat: Use full-size hat pattern and cut two hat sections from felt remnant. Stitch hat sections along curved edge. Trim lower edge with pinking shears. Turn; fold up brim. Cut six 6" lengths of floss. Knot together at center; trim floss ends to make pom-pom. Stitch pom-pom to top of hat. Cut two 3" pieces of floss; glue inside lower edge of hat at seams to make ties.

Finishing: Place vest on kid. If desired, overlap and glue front edges of vest. If desired, cut a bow tie shape from felt and stitch edges with optional running stitches; glue bow to kid. Sew 8" of floss through hat or top of head for hanging loop; knot floss ends.

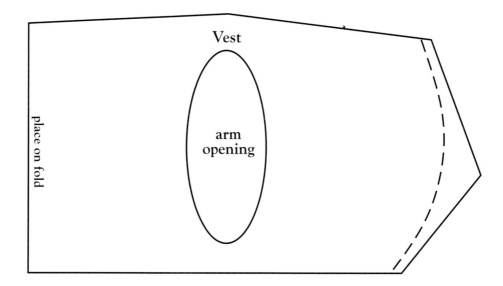

Hat

Body

terrific tables (pages 52-61)

WOODEN TREE

You need: 1 recipe Tree and Animal Cookie Dough (page 101); drinking straw; small cookie cutters; 6' of 1/4" beaded molding; saw; 6" square of 1/2" thick pine (base); drill with 1/16" bit; screwdriver; 1" screw; 18" of 1/2" x 3/4" pine (trunk); hot-glue gun with wood-glue sticks; paintbrush; green acrylic paint; green floral wire; wired paper cord – red, green striped.

Cutting: Cut the following lengths from beading for tree branches – 3", 4", 5", 6", 8", 10", 12", 14".

Assembling tree: Drill screw-guide hole in center of base and center bottom of trunk; attach trunk to base with screw. Starting near top of trunk with smallest branch, glue branches to trunk; space branches about 2" apart to make tree.

Making cookies: Roll out dough as directed in recipe. Cut with small cookie cutters. Place cookies 1" apart on baking sheet. Using straw, poke two holes in center of each cookie. Bake and cool according to recipe.

Decorating tree: Paint tree and base green. Cut 10" pieces of wired paper cord; slip through cookie holes. Coil cord ends around tree branches. Attach cookie cutters to branches with floral wire.

GINGHAM CHAIR PADS

You need (for each pad): Tracing paper; 3/4 yd each of green and red checked fabric; 3 yds 1/4" cotton cord; 1/2" thick foam pad, cut to size of chair seat; 1 wood star ornament and 2 jingle bells (optional).

Making pattern: Place tracing paper on chair; draw around seat edges to mark pad shape. Add 1/2" to outline all around to make pad pattern.

Cutting: *From green fabric* – Cut two pad sections. *From red fabric* – cut two 3" x 22" ties. Cut remaining red fabric into 2"W bias strips; piece strips, end to end, to make continuous strip for piping.

Making piping: Fold piping strip, right sides out, over cord; stitch close to cord.

Making pad: Pin piping to edge of one pad section; stitch 1/2" seam. Pin pad sections with right sides facing; stitch 1/2" seams, leaving one side open. Turn; insert foam. Slipstitch opening closed.

Finishing: Fold each tie in half lengthwise, right sides together; stitch all edges, leaving opening along long edge. Turn; slipstitch opening closed. Hand stitch center of each tie to back corner of pad. If desired, slip ornament on one ties and bells onto other tie.

GINGERBREAD COTTAGE

You need: Lightweight cardboard; rolling pin; 1 recipe Gingerbread Cookie Mitts dough (page 94); craft knife; pastry bag with assorted tips; 3 recipes of Royal Icing (page 94) – 1 left white, 1 tinted green, 1 tinted red; aluminum foil; butter; 1 cup sugar; assorted candies – 5 peppermint sticks, chocolate-coated crunchy candy, red and green gumdrops, red and green sour balls, peppermint disks, red-, white-, and green-coated candy balls, peppermint balls, red and green jelly rings.

Making cottage pieces: Enlarge patterns; cut from cardboard. Roll out dough to 1/4" thick. Place patterns on dough; cut around pattern edges with craft knife. Remove excess dough around pieces. Cut out windows; remove dough from inside windows (cut into pieces for window boxes). Cut out door. Mark heart in door with knife; do not remove dough from inside heart. Transfer all pieces to baking sheet; bake according to recipe. Let cool.

Assembling base: Fit pastry bag with fine tip; fill with white icing. Place front, back, and two side cottage sections on end; pipe icing where pieces meet to form cottage base.

Making windows: Coat foil with butter. Melt sugar in non-stick frying pan over very low heat, stirring constantly. When sugar begins to brown, remove from heat; pour onto buttered foil in thin layer. When sugar cools, break into pieces large enough to fit in windows, for stained glass. Pipe icing around edges of each piece of glass; press behind each window or door cutout.

Attaching roof: Place one roof section on cottage; pipe icing along side edges to attach. Place remaining roof section on cottage; pipe icing along side edges and at roof peak.

Decorating: *Pipe white icing where candies are to be adhered, unless noted; refer to photo for candy placement; press candy firmly into icing.* Adhere peppermint sticks at corner edges and along one side of doorway. Adhere window boxes below windows. Pipe large amount of icing along center of one side of house; adhere crunchy candy here to form chimney. Adhere gum drops along lower edges of house front and back, alternating colors. Adhere sour balls along lower edges of house sides, alternating colors. Pipe green or red icing around each sour ball. Pipe white icing around each window, and across center of each piece of stained glass. Pipe white icing onto roof; press peppermint disks into icing for shingles. Pipe icing onto each shingle; press one candy ball into icing on each shingle. Pipe icing on roof at top of chimney; press crunchy candy into icing. Make chimney desired height by adding layers of icing and candy. Pipe icing stripes and dots on door. Pipe green icing and red dots around edge of roof. Pipe white-icing icicles by touching pastry tip to edge of roof, then slowly squeezing out icing.

Finishing: Pipe icing details and adhere remaining candies as desired.

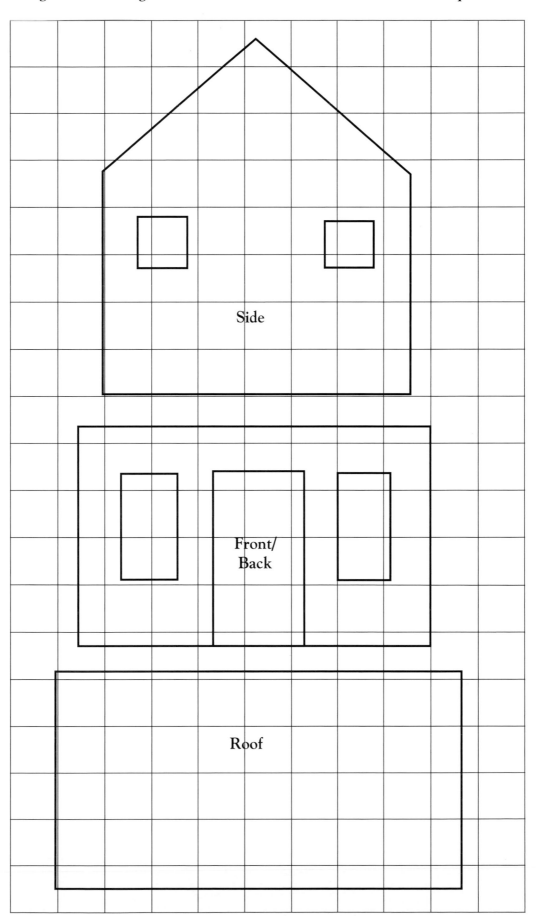

Side

Front/
Back

Roof

NO-SEW ADVENT BANNER (continued)

Attaching hanging loops: Cut two 10" lengths of 1 1/2"W ribbon. Use web tape to fuse ends of each ribbon length together to form loops; fuse loops to back of banner.

Finishing: Thread bell onto remaining 1 1/2"W ribbon; tie ribbon in bow. Glue bow to banner.

Small Heart

Large Heart

Hurry Santa!

PEPPERMINT KISSING BALL

You need: 6" of ¹/₄"W ribbon; glue gun; 4" plastic foam ball; 2 gumdrop rings; peppermints; green and red candies.
Note: Ball is for decorative use only. Do not eat.
Assembling: Fold ribbon in half to make hanging loop; glue to top of ball. Thread gumdrop rings over loop. Glue unwrapped peppermints to ball. Glue green and red candies to mints.

REDWORK STAR ORNAMENT

You need: Two 8" squares of white fabric; red embroidery floss; tracing paper; iron-on transfer pen; fiberfill; 6" of ¹/₈"W red satin ribbon.
Preparing pattern: Trace full-size pattern onto tracing paper. Use transfer pen to transfer pattern to one fabric square.
Embroidering: *Use two strands of floss.* Work straight stitches for pine needles, running stitches for dash lines, outline stitch for remaining solid lines, and French knots for dots.
Making ornament: Place fabric squares right sides together. Stitch pieces together ¹/₄" from outer stitching, leaving opening; trim seam to ¹/₈"; turn. Stuff; sew closed.
Finishing: Cut twenty-five 6" lengths of floss. Hold lengths together; knot a length of floss around center. Fold floss in half at knot. Tie another length around folded floss ¹/₂" from fold to form tassel. Stitch tassel to bottom of star. Stitch ends of ribbon to top of star to form hanging loop.

STRIPED FLOWER POTS

You need (for each pot): Small terra-cotta pot; sponge paintbrushes; acrylic paints – white, crimson; ¹/₂"W masking tape; antiquing medium – medium brown; soft cloth.
Painting: Paint pot white; let dry. Apply masking-tape stripes to pot. Paint pot crimson; peel off tape. Let dry.
Antiquing: Coat pot with antiquing medium. While still wet, wipe off excess with soft cloth. Let dry.

POLKA-DOT TEAPOT

You need: Wooden teapot; sandpaper; sponge paintbrush; acrylic paints – red, white; 1" round white stickers; matte acrylic sealer.
Note: Teapot is for decorative purposes only. Do not use for beverages.
Painting: Sand teapot. Paint teapot red and knob and feet white; let dry.
Finishing: Apply stickers to pot. Coat with sealer; let dry.

Redwork Star

PARTY POPS

Non-stick vegetable-oil cooking spray
8 straight-sided 3-inch metal cookie cutters
8 lollipop sticks
3/4 cup water
1 1/2 cups sugar
3/4 cup light corn syrup
2 teaspoons unsalted butter
1/4 teaspoon cinnamon oil OR peppermint oil
Red food coloring (for red pops only)
1 recipe of Royal Icing (page 94)
Hot-cinnamon candies

Preparing pans: Line 2 large baking sheets with foil. Spray foil and cookie cutters liberally with cooking spray. Place 4 cutters on each pan about 3" apart. Place lollipop sticks nearby.
Making lollipops: Combine water, sugar, corn syrup, and butter in a 3-quart saucepan. Heat over medium heat, stirring occasionally, until sugar is dissolved. Increase heat; bring to a boil. Cover and cook for 3 minutes. Uncover; boil without stirring until mixture reaches 310° on candy thermometer, about 20 minutes. Remove from heat; stir in flavoring and food coloring. Let stand 8 to 10 minutes to cool mixture slightly. Do not let harden. Using metal 1/4-cup measure with long handle, scoop warm mixture and pour into prepared cutters. Let cool 4 to 5 minutes. While lollipops are somewhat soft, carefully slip off cutters and quickly press lollipop sticks into shapes. Let cool completely; trim away any rough edges with paring knife.
Decorating: Spoon icing into pastry bag fitted with a #2 round tip. Pipe designs; press candies into wet icing.
Yield: Makes 8 pops

FROSTED VOTIVES

You need (for each votive): Glass votive; masking tape; adhesive dots and stars; rubber gloves; paintbrush; glass-etching cream.
Preparing glass: Wash and dry votive. Apply tape, dots, and stars to outside of votive as desired.
Etching glass: Wear rubber gloves. Following manufacturer's directions, brush a coat of etching cream onto glass. Allow to set for 10 to 15 minutes; rinse. Remove tape, dots, and stars; wash votive.

SCALLOPED RUNNER

You need: 2 1/4 yds each of fabric and lining; transfer paper; cardboard; dressmaker's pencil; 7 yds piping.
Marking: Cut 78" x 16" piece each of fabric and lining. Enlarge pattern; transfer onto cardboard to make template. Fold fabric lengthwise. Place template in corner of fabric, with dotted line along fold. Draw outline of template onto fabric. Repeat at opposite end. Using template scallops as guide, draw scallops along long raw edge of fabric.
Cutting: Cut fabric along marked lines through both layers. Open out fabric; use as pattern to cut lining.
Assembling: Baste piping to right side of fabric. Pin lining to fabric, right sides facing. Stitch with 1/4" seam, leaving small opening. Clip curves; turn. Slipstitch opening closed.

Scalloped Runner

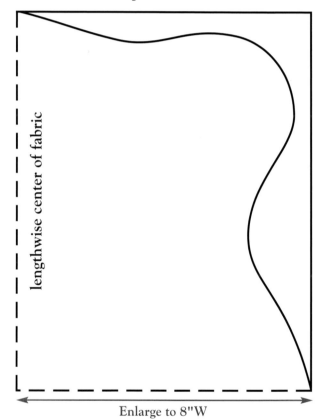

lengthwise center of fabric

Enlarge to 8"W

KRIS KRINGLE KRACKERS

You need (for each cracker): Paper-towel tube, cut to 4½" long; candies; decorative-edge scissors; tissue paper – white, red; craft glue; 12" of ribbon; star-shaped hole punch.

Making cracker: Cut one 8" x 10" piece of white paper and one 8" square of red paper using decorative-edge scissors. Wrap and glue white paper, then red paper, around tube. Fill tube with candy. Cut ribbon in half; tie around ends. Cut 1½" square of white paper; punch star in center. Glue to cracker.

BIRCH-BARK NAPKIN RING

You need: Birch bark, about 2" x 13" (use bark strips that have peeled away naturally from tree and have fallen to the ground; do not peel loose bark from tree); woodburning tool; glue gun; pinking shears; two hemlock cones.

To do: Print name on one end of bark strip with woodburning tool. Fold strip in half; glue ends together, leaving a 3" loop (for napkin). Trim short ends evenly with pinking shears. Glue two hemlock cones to loop.

HAND-PAINTED SLEIGH

You need: Kraft paper sleigh; acrylic paints – red, black, white, brown, green, yellow; flat paintbrush; stencil brush; plastic stencils — trees, snowflakes, bear, stars, moon; assorted brown buttons; two white buttons; glue gun.

Painting: Paint sleigh red, runners black. Add white stripes along rim.

Stenciling: Stencil white snowflakes on runners. Stencil trees, bear, stars, and moon on sides.

Finishing: Paint a large freehand tree on sleigh front. Glue white buttons to front panel (like "headlamps"), and brown buttons in a row along front rim and singly at corners of sides.

STAR CANDLE HOLDERS

You need (for each): Star-shaped wooden candle holder; acrylic paints – colors of your choice; paintbrushes; holiday-motif fabric; scissors; decoupage medium; embellishments (e.g., small wooden stars, buttons); glue gun.

Painting: Paint edges of holder and cutout "candle cup" as desired.

Decoupaging: Cut up fabric for a patchwork to cover top of candle holder (except for the center circle over "candle cup"). Brush decoupage medium on wrong side of fabric; adhere to top of candle holder. When dry, brush one to two coats decoupage medium over fabric, drying between applications. If necessary, paint wooden stars, buttons. When dry, glue embellishments to fabric.

CHAIR-BACK DECORATIONS

You need (for each): Red ribbon, yarn, or raffia; pinecone; glue gun; sprig of fresh pine.

To do: Cut a length of ribbon to span chair back, plus extra inches to tie on to back spindles. Glue pinecone to midpoint of ribbon; tuck in pine sprig (dot with glue if needed to secure). Tie ribbon to spindles so decoration falls in mid-back of chair.

basic how-to's

Embroidery

Blanket Stitch

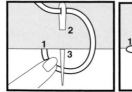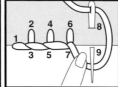

French Knot

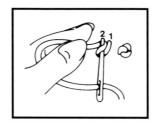

Herringbone Stitch

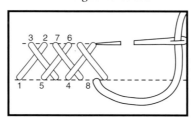

Running Stitch

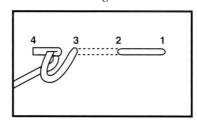

Satin Stitch

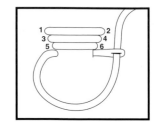

Straight Stitch

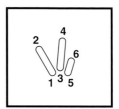

Outline Stitch

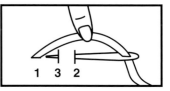

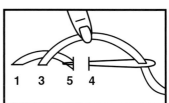

Cross Stitch

Cross Stitch

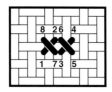

¼ Cross Stitch

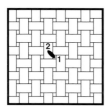

Backstitch

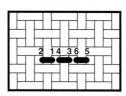

Crochet and Knit Abbreviations

beg – beginning
ch(s) – chain(s)
dc – double crochet
dec – decrease
dp – double–pointed
gr – grams
inc – increase

k – knit
mm – millimeters
p – purl
patt – pattern
r/s – right side
rem – remaining
rnd(s) – round(s)

sc – single crochet
sk – skein
skp – skip
sp – space
St st – Stockinette stitch
st(s) – stitch(es)
tog – together

tr – treble
w/s – wrong side
yds – yards
YO – yarn over